Vocabulary in Context
FOR THE COMMON CORE STANDARDS

Grade 5

Table of Contents

Introduction 4
Word Lists 5

Unit 1
Egyptian Tomb Discovered 8
Context Clues 9
Word Groups 10
Cloze Paragraph 10
Crossword Puzzle 11
Dictionary Skills 12
Standardized Test Practice 13
Word Parts 14
Analogies 15
Explore Word Meanings 16
Writing 17

Unit 2
Treasures from the Deep 18
Context Clues 19
Word Origins 20
Cloze Paragraph 20
Word Map 21
Tangled-Up Words 22
Standardized Test Practice 23
Synonyms 24
Latin Roots 25
Words in Context 25
Multiple-Meaning Words 26
Writing 27

Unit 3
Tarahumara Racers 28
Context Clues 29
Challenge Yourself 29
Synonyms 30
Dictionary Skills 30
Analogies 31
Writing Sentences 31
Crossword Puzzle 32
Standardized Test Practice 33
Explore Word Meanings 34

Synonyms/Antonyms 35
Word Origins/Etymology 36
Writing 37

Unit 4
Icarus and Daedalus 38
Context Clues 40
Challenge Yourself 40
Synonyms 41
Antonyms 41
Figurative Language 42
Standardized Test Practice 43
Rhyming Words 44
Using Synonyms 45
Confusing Words 46
Writing 47

Unit 5
Walking in Space 48
Context Clues 49
Challenge Yourself 49
Word Sense 50
Synonyms 50
Crossword Puzzle 51
Related Words 52
Writing Sentences 52
Standardized Test Practice 53
Greek Roots 54
Compare and Contrast 54
Using Related Words 55
Acronyms 56
Writing 57

Unit 6
Marvelous Jackie Robinson 58
Context Clues 59
Related Words 60
Writing Sentences 60
Tangled-Up Words 61
Word Sense 62
Word Pairs 62

Standardized Test Practice 63
Synonyms and Antonyms 64
Multiple-Meaning Words 65
Using Context Clues 66
Writing 67

Unit 7
A Well-Ordered World 68
Context Clues..69
Writing Sentences 70
Cloze Paragraphs 70
Word Map 71
Word Sense 72
Challenge Yourself.....................................72
Standardized Test Practice 73
Word Endings 74
Using Context Clues 75
Antonyms 76
Writing 77

Unit 8
Insect Self-Defense 78
Context Clues..79
Word Groups..80
Challenge Yourself.....................................80
Word Sense 81
Word Pairs 81
Dictionary Skills...82
Standardized Test Practice 83
Word Families 84
Analogies 85
Suffixes 86
Writing 87

Unit 9
Spiders Are Builders 88
Context Clues..89
Challenge Yourself.....................................89
Analogies 90
Writing Sentences 90
Hidden Message Puzzle............................91

Yes or No?...92
Standardized Test Practice 93
Content-Area Words..................................94
Related Words 95
Compare and Contrast...............................96
Writing 97

Unit 10
Real Art? 98
Context Clues..99
Challenge Yourself.....................................99
Antonyms 100
Rewriting Sentences................................100
Related Words 101
Word Sense 101
Crossword Puzzle....................................102
Standardized Test Practice 103
Compare and Contrast.............................104
Related Words 105
Classify/Categorize 106
Writing 107

Glossary 108

Answer Key 117

Introduction

Steck-Vaughn's *Vocabulary in Context* series offers parents and educators high-quality, curriculum-based products that align with the Common Core Standards for English Language Arts for grades 2–9.

Each unit in the *Vocabulary in Context* books includes:

- fiction and/or nonfiction selections, covering a wide variety of topics

- context activities, ascertaining that students understand what they have read

- vocabulary activities, challenging students to show their understanding of key vocabulary

- questions in a standardized-test format, helping prepare students for standardized exams

- word skills activities, targeting additional vocabulary words and vocabulary skills

- writing activities, providing assignments that encourage students to use the vocabulary words

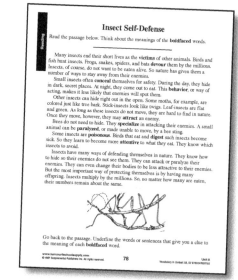

Reading selection

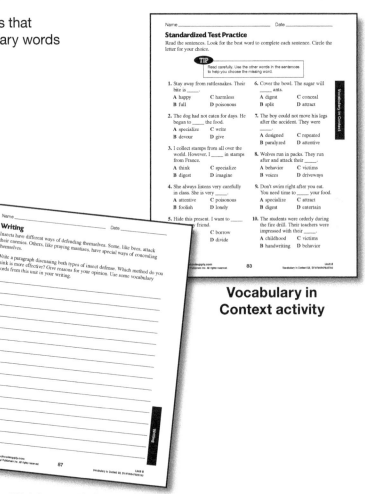

Vocabulary in Context activity

Word Skills activity

Writing activity

Homophones

Homophones are words that sound the same but have different meanings and usually have different spellings.

ant—aunt	groan—grown	right—write
ate—eight	heal—heel	road—rode—rowed
base—bass	here—hear	sail—sale
be—bee	hi—high	sea—see
beach—beech	hoarse—horse	seen—scene
bear—bare	hole—whole	sew—so—sow
beat—beet	hour—our	sight—cite—site
berry—bury	I—eye	some—sum
blew—blue	made—maid	son—sun
bored—board	meat—meet	sore—soar
bow—bough	new—knew	stair—stare
brake—break	no—know	steal—steel
buy—by	oar—or	their—there—they're
cell—sell	one—won	through—threw
cent—sent—scent	pail—pale	to—too—two
close—clothes	pain—pane	wail—whale
dear—deer	pair—pear	weak—week
flew—flu	peace—piece	we'll—wheel
flour—flower	peek—peak	wait—weight
for—four	plane—plain	way—weigh
forth—fourth	principal—principle	wood—would

Homographs

Homographs are words that are spelled the same but have different meanings and different origins (*bat*—the mammal, *bat*—the club). Some homographs also have different pronunciations (*august*—majestic, *August*—eighth month).

close	shut / near
dove	pigeon / did dive
live	to exist / having life
desert	abandon / arid land
object	thing / disagree
record	to make note of / best achievement
tear	rip / drop of water from an eye
refuse	to say no / trash
lead	heavy metal / to be first
does	form of *do* / female deer

Prefixes

Prefixes are letter groups added before a base word to change or add to the word's meaning.

Prefix	Meaning	Example
auto-	self	autobiography
bi-	two	bicycle, biweekly
dis-	not	disbelief
im-	not	impossible
in-	into, not	inside, independence
non-	not	nonfiction
pre-	before	prehistoric
re-	again	resend
tele-	far	telescope
trans-	across	transportation
tri-	three	triangle
uni-	one	unify

Suffixes

Suffixes are letter groups added after a base word to change or add to the word's meaning.

Suffix	Meaning	Example
-er	one who	teacher
-er	more	brighter
-est	most	brightest
-ful	full of	wonderful
-ing	(present tense)	smiling
-less	without	penniless
-ling	small	duckling
-ly	every	weekly
-ly	(adverb)	quickly
-ness	state of being	happiness
-or	one who	actor
-y	state of	funny

Egyptian Tomb Discovered

Read the passage below. Think about the meanings of the **boldfaced** words.

Gleaming gold statues, secret treasures, and other objects are all **artifacts**. They tell of a group of people who lived long ago. **Archaeologists** who study such people dreamed of finding these objects in Egypt in the early 1900s. These experts hoped to learn about an ancient **civilization**.

When Egyptian kings died long ago, they were placed in **tombs**. Some tombs were as large as houses. They contained **chambers**, or rooms, where the king and his treasures were buried. Archaeologists searched for these tombs. But all the graves found had been robbed long ago. Only the tomb of King Tutankhamen was still to be found in the area of the **pyramids**, those huge buildings made from stone.

Howard Carter, an archaeologist, was eager to find this tomb. Lord Carnarvon, a rich Englishman, gave Carter the money for the **expedition**. So Carter went to Egypt.

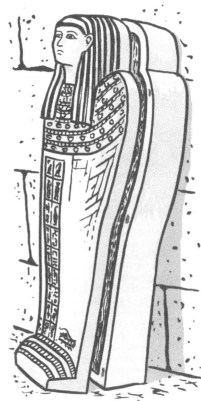

In 1922, Carter's search led him to an ancient entrance. He believed it led to Tutankhamen's tomb. Carter wanted to **investigate** what he had found with Carnarvon. So he sent Carnarvon a letter telling him to come. Together they would closely examine the tomb.

Three weeks later, Carter and Carnarvon were ready to share the **historic** moment when the door to the tomb was opened. It was an important time in history. Carter carefully cut a hole in the door that had been sealed for over three thousand years. Then he held a candle inside the tomb. Carter and Carnarvon saw many riches, including beautiful carved and gold-covered objects. Both were certain that beyond these objects lay King Tutankhamen. It was **evident** that they had found the right tomb.

Go back to the passage. Underline the words or sentences that give you a clue to the meaning of each **boldfaced** word.

Name _____   Date _____

Context Clues

Read each pair of sentences. Look for a clue in the first sentence to help you choose the missing word in the second sentence. Write the word from the box that completes each sentence.

| archaeologists | chambers | investigate | artifacts | historic |
| civilization | evident | tombs | pyramids | expedition |

1. Some scientists study how people lived long ago. These scientists are called _____.

2. Long ago, a group of people lived in Egypt. That _____ created many beautiful objects.

3. Carter wanted to travel to Egypt to find treasures. He was eager to start his_____.

4. In ancient times, it was difficult to build with massive stones. That is why the _____ amaze us.

5. Egyptian kings were buried in special graves. These _____ were in the desert.

6. A tomb may have several rooms. In one of these _____, the king is buried.

7. Carter couldn't wait to examine the tomb. At last it was time to _____.

8. Discovering the tomb was important. Seeing King Tutankhamen would be a _____ moment.

9. Carter uncovered many precious objects. Some of these _____ were statues and jewels.

10. It was easy to see that Carter was delighted. His joy was _____.

Name _____ Date _____

Word Groups

Read each pair of words. Think about how they are alike. Write the word from the box that best completes each group.

> expedition   archaeologist   tomb

1. grave, memorial, _____
2. builder, teacher, _____
3. journey, trip, _____

Cloze Paragraph

Use the words in the box to complete the paragraph. Read the paragraph again to be sure it makes sense.

> artifacts   historic   expedition   tomb
> archaeologists   investigated   civilization evident

Less than five months after the opening of King Tutankhamen's (1) _____, Lord Carnarvon died. Carter had not yet (2) _____ far enough into the tomb to find the king, so Carnarvon never saw Tutankhamen's true resting place. Carnarvon's death caused him to miss the (3) _____ moment when Tutankhamen's golden mask was seen for the first time in thousands of years. The ancient Egyptian (4) _____ produced not only this beautiful object but other remarkable (5) _____ as well. (6) _____ everywhere were amazed. One thing was (7) _____. The discoveries from Carter's (8) _____ would remain one of the world's greatest treasures.

Crossword Puzzle

Use the clues and the words in the box to complete the crossword puzzle.

| expedition | evident | chambers | tombs | archaeologists |
| artifacts | historic | investigate | pyramids | civilization |

Across

1. to examine closely
4. scientists who study the people and customs of ancient times
5. huge ancient stone buildings in Egypt
6. places to be buried; graves
7. rooms
8. group of people who live during a certain time and place
9. famous or important in history

Down

2. easy to see or understand
3. a journey for a specific purpose
4. products of human skill

Name _____ Date _____

Dictionary Skills

Guide words are the two words at the top of each dictionary page. They show the first and last entries on that page. All the word entries in between are in alphabetical order. Look at the pairs of guide words. On the lines below each pair, write the words from the box that would appear on the same dictionary page. Be sure to put them in alphabetical order.

| tombs | chambers | evident | expedition | investigate |
| historic | artifacts | archaeologists | civilization | pyramids |

1. ant/jump

2. lemon/uneven

Now choose one word from each column. Write an original sentence using each word.

3. _____

4. _____

Name _____ Date _____

Standardized Test Practice

Circle the letter for the word or words that have the same or almost the same meaning as the boldfaced word.

Be sure to mark the answer correctly. Do not circle the word. Circle the letter neatly with your pencil.

1. to **investigate** a mystery
   - A invite
   - B forget
   - C write about
   - D search into

2. the **tombs** of kings
   - A graves
   - B bedrooms
   - C thrones
   - D palaces

3. a **chamber** in the castle
   - A floor
   - B room
   - C stranger
   - D ghost

4. a jungle **expedition**
   - A tree
   - B animal
   - C experiment
   - D trip

5. an **evident** clue
   - A hidden
   - B written
   - C easy to see
   - D hard to read

6. a group of **archaeologists**
   - A scientists
   - B kings
   - C actors
   - D tourists

7. a **historic** moment
   - A important
   - B common
   - C funny
   - D heroic

8. an ancient **civilization**
   - A disease
   - B group of people
   - C tomb
   - D way of travel

9. build **pyramids**
   - A crowded villages
   - B rough shacks
   - C small houses
   - D huge buildings

10. **artifacts** discovered
    - A secrets
    - B languages
    - C objects
    - D people

Vocabulary in Context

Name _____ Date _____

Word Parts

Knowing the meanings of prefixes, suffixes, and roots can help you figure out the meanings of unfamiliar words. Use the prefixes, roots, and suffix in the box, as well as your own knowledge, to help you write a definition for each of the following words.

Prefix/Meaning	Root/Meaning	Suffix/Meaning
mis- badly, poorly, not *socio-* group of people	*anthrop* human *archae* ancient *log* study *phil* like, love	*-ist* one who is or does

1. anthropologist _____
2. archaeologist _____
3. misanthrope _____
4. philanthropist _____
5. sociologist _____

Now use your knowledge of prefixes, suffixes, and roots to answer the following questions.

6. Which city's name means "city of brotherly love," Chicago or Philadelphia? How can you tell?

   _____

   _____

7. What would the study of ancient civilizations be called? _____

8. What part or parts of the word *Egyptologist* tell you that an Egyptologist is a scientist?

   _____

Name _____ Date _____

Analogies

An **analogy** shows a relationship between two pairs of words or terms.

Canvas is to *artist* as *camera* is to *photographer.*

Write a word to complete each analogy.

1. *Naturalist* is to *natural history* as _____ is to *Egypt.*

2. *Misanthrope* is to *philanthropist* as *hate* is to _____.

3. *Geologist* is to *Earth* as *anthropologist* is to _____.

4. *Leaves* are to *botanist* as *artifacts* are to _____.

5. A *comedian* is to *comedy* as a *historian* is to _____.

6. A *sociologist* is to *groups of people* as a *zoologist* is to _____.

7. *Letters* are to *words* as *digits* are to _____.

8. *Lamp* is to *electricity* as *flashlight* is to _____.

9. *Ant* is to *colony* as *bird* is to _____.

10. *Three* is to *triangle* as *four* is to _____.

11. *Optometry* is to *eyes* as *podiatry* is to _____.

12. *Carnivore* is to *meat* as *herbivore* is to _____.

13. *Ice* is to *solid* as *lemonade* is to _____.

14. *Basket* is to *straw* as *sweater* is to _____.

15. *Urban* is to *rural* as *city* is to _____.

Name _____   Date _____

Explore Word Meanings

Read and respond to each of the following questions. Use complete sentences.

1. What are some things a *philanthropist* might do?

   _____
   _____

2. What things might an *Egyptologist* study on a trip to Egypt?

   _____
   _____

3. Why are *historians* important? _____

   _____

4. Is it likely that a *misanthrope* would be a *sociologist*? Why or why not?

   _____
   _____

5. Would an *archaeologist* be interested in studying the history of the Second World War? Why or why not?

   _____
   _____

6. What do *anthropologists* and *sociologists* have in common?

   _____
   _____

Name _____ Date _____

Writing

Howard Carter and Lord Carnarvon were determined to find the tomb of King Tutankhamen. Have you or someone you know ever worked hard to achieve a difficult goal?

Write a paragraph discussing this goal. What was the goal? Was help needed? Was the goal achieved? Use some vocabulary words from this unit in your writing.

Treasures from the Deep

Read the passage below. Think about the meanings of the **boldfaced** words.

On a sunny September morning in 1622, a fleet of 28 ships set sail from Cuba. Their **destination** was Spain. The ships had come to America to gather riches for King Philip. Now they were headed home with treasure. Before two days had passed, however, the ships were hit by a howling hurricane. Most of the ships were sunk off the coast of Florida. Their crews and their treasures were lost beneath the waves.

Over the years, many treasure hunters searched for the **sunken** *Atocha*. This ship was known to have carried most of the treasures. Yet it was not until 1972 that the *Atocha* was found. The **discoverers** were Mel Fisher and Bob Holloway. They had worked for more than five years to find the ship.

It is not an easy task to search for **undersea** treasure. Through the years, the ocean had wrecked the ship and buried the **hull**. The ship's body was under shifting sands. Fisher and Holloway used two boats in their search. They had to **navigate**, or steer, their boats through rough waters. At times the swelling waves hit the ships. These **billows** filled them with water.

The two search boats carried different equipment. Holloway's boat carried magnets that could find metal far below the surface. When magnets showed **evidence** of metal, Holloway threw a **buoy** into the water. This was a signal to Fisher. Now Fisher knew where he and his team should go to work. The second boat carried digging tools and diving gear. Fisher told his **scuba** divers to get ready. They put on wet suits and air tanks and slipped into the water.

The first dives were disappointing. But then one day, a diver burst to the surface. In his hand were gold necklaces! This was only the beginning. Divers found gold coins and bars of silver. They found cups decorated with emeralds. The *Atocha* had released its treasure from the deep at last!

Go back to the passage. Underline the words or sentences that give you a clue to the meaning of each **boldfaced** word.

Name _____   Date _____

Context Clues

Read each pair of sentences. Look for a clue in the first sentence to help you choose the missing word in the second sentence. Write the word from the box that completes each sentence.

> discoverers   sunken   undersea   hull   destination
> billows   buoy   scuba   navigate   evidence

1. In 1622, the *Atocha* sank beneath the sea. The _____ ship remained hidden for 350 years.

2. The ship had set out for Spain. This _____ was its home country.

3. The sailors knew how to handle the ship. But they could not _____ it through a hurricane.

4. The sails and rigging of the *Atocha* were torn away. Only the _____ was left, and it soon sank.

5. Centuries later, people found clues to the location of the lost ship. Now there was real _____.

6. The men who found the *Atocha* worked secretly. These _____ wanted to protect their find.

7. A weighted floating object was used as a signal. The _____ marked a possible treasure site.

8. Working underwater requires careful planning. An _____ job is not easy.

9. Divers worked from small boats despite the huge waves. These _____ nearly overturned the boats.

10. The divers used special breathing equipment. The _____ equipment made their work easier.

Name _____ Date _____

Word Origins

A **word origin** is the history of a word. Knowing where a word comes from can help you understand its meaning. Read each word origin. Then write each word from the box in front of its origin.

> evidence   hull   navigate   scuba

1. from Latin *navis*, ship, and *iglare*, to drive _____

2. from Dutch *hol*, hold _____

3. from Latin *videre*, to see _____

4. first letters of its description:
   self-contained underwater breathing apparatus _____

Cloze Paragraph

Use the words in the box to complete the paragraph. Read the paragraph again to be sure it makes sense.

> discoverers   buoy   sunken
> billows   destination undersea

Lots of treasure may be hidden (1) _____. But in the search

for a (2) _____ ship, divers have to worry about such threats

as sharks. Divers also have to be concerned about strong winds and

(3) _____ of waves. A (4) _____ is often used

as a marker so that divers can find their (5) _____, the place

where the treasure lies. If divers become (6) _____ of treasure,

their hard work will have been rewarded.

Name _____ Date _____

Word Map

Use the vocabulary words in the box to complete the word map about buried treasure. Add other words that you know to each group. One heading will not have any vocabulary words, but only your words.

| sunken | discoverers | scuba |
| undersea | buoy | |

1. Who Finds Treasure
_____
_____
_____
_____

2. Where Treasure Is Found
_____
_____
_____
_____

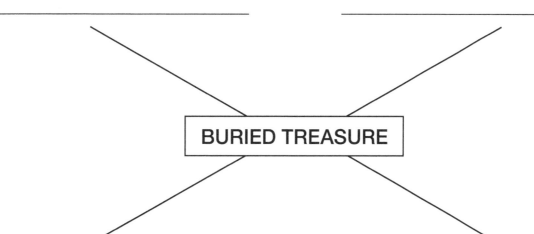

BURIED TREASURE

3. Things Used to Hunt Treasure
_____
_____
_____
_____

4. Kinds of Treasure Found
_____
_____
_____
_____

Name _____   Date _____

Tangled-Up Words

A word is underlined in each sentence below. The word sounds similar to a word in the box. But its meaning makes it the wrong word for the sentence.

Read the paragraph. Find the word in the box that should replace the underlined word. Write the word on the line next to the number of the underlined word.

| discoverers | sunken | undersea | hull | destination |
| billows | buoy | scuba | navigate | evidence |

   I learned how to (1) scooter dive this summer. I started in a pool, and I was attached to a (2) boy. Soon I could (3) native easily through the water. I felt like an (4) underneath explorer. Finally, we went out in the ocean. Our (5) declaration was a (6) dunking shipwreck. (7) Discolored found it years ago. No (8) residence of treasure remains, but we could see a big part of the ship's (9) hole. It must have taken huge (10) pillows to sink a ship like that.

1. _____
2. _____
3. _____
4. _____
5. _____
6. _____
7. _____
8. _____
9. _____
10. _____

Name _____ Date _____

Standardized Test Practice

Read the sentences. Look for the best word to complete each sentence. Circle the letter for your choice.

> **TIP**
> If you are not sure which word completes the sentence, do the best you can. Try to choose the answer that makes the most sense.

1. The treasure lay at the bottom of the ocean. It was in a _____ ship.
   - **A** foreign
   - **B** sunken
   - **C** scuba
   - **D** new

2. The search team set out. Their _____ was the Florida coast.
   - **A** destination
   - **B** evidence
   - **C** discoverer
   - **D** buoy

3. They used underwater equipment. This _____ gear allowed them to breathe.
   - **A** space
   - **B** camping
   - **C** scuba
   - **D** sunken

4. Parts of the ship had been destroyed. The _____ lay on the ocean floor.
   - **A** billows
   - **B** watch
   - **C** fish
   - **D** hull

5. The crew had tried to save the ship. They could not _____ through a storm.
   - **A** argue
   - **B** navigate
   - **C** agree
   - **D** discover

6. The weather sank the ship. It was turned over by wind and strong _____.
   - **A** evidence
   - **B** billows
   - **C** rafts
   - **D** rocks

7. The divers got ready. They were prepared for their _____ mission.
   - **A** shiny
   - **B** high
   - **C** undersea
   - **D** careless

8. They looked for proof of the ship. They found the _____ they wanted.
   - **A** evidence
   - **B** billows
   - **C** magic
   - **D** discoverers

9. They used a marker to locate the ship. This _____ floated on top of the water.
   - **A** destination
   - **B** swimmer
   - **C** billow
   - **D** buoy

10. They found the treasure. As the _____, they were allowed to keep it.
    - **A** sailors
    - **B** discoverers
    - **C** billows
    - **D** losers

Vocabulary in Context

Name _____ Date _____

Synonyms

Synonyms are words that have the same or nearly the same meaning. Underline the pair of synonyms in each row. Consult the glossary or a dictionary if you need help.

1. stimulus	response	incentive	effort
2. peacefulness	motive	reason	confidence
3. point	prod	pull	goad
4. catalyst	speaker	incentive	aim
5. discourage	prompt	prevent	urge
6. recreation	recommendation	provocation	incitation
7. needless	required	unnecessary	dependable
8. unknowing	cunning	sly	disrespectful
9. magnificent	simple	luxury	splendid
10. donate	possess	own	reply
11. energetic	funny	tired	exhausted
12. disease	wellness	illness	scornful
13. clouds	precipitation	sunny	rain
14. peace	busy	piece	part
15. grow	shrink	water	flourish
16. weak	strong	powerful	cheerful
17. performer	doctor	painter	dancer
18. create	conduct	ruin	destroy

Name _____ Date _____

Latin Roots

In each of the following words, explain how the Latin root supports the definition of the English word.

1. *incentive* from the Latin root meaning "to set the tune" _____
_____
_____

2. *prompt* from the Latin root meaning "to bring forth" _____
_____
_____

3. *motive* from the Latin root meaning "to move" _____
_____
_____

Words in Context

Complete each phrase with the appropriate word from the box.

| catalyst | stimulus | motive | incentive |

1. a/an _____ for learning

2. a/an _____ for change

3. provide a/an _____ for creativity

4. a/an _____ for the crime

Name _____ Date _____

Multiple-Meaning Words

Some words have more than one meaning. Clues tell you which meaning is being used. Determine how the underlined word is used in each phrase. Circle the letter of the correct definition. Then write a sentence using the definition you didn't circle.

1. goad you into finishing the project
   A a sharp pointed stick for driving oxen
   B to urge someone on

   _____

2. have a motive for doing well
   A a main idea or element
   B an impulse or inner reason

   _____

3. prod him to do well
   A to jab with a stick
   B to urge and encourage

   _____

4. to prompt an actor with his lines
   A to help or support
   B to be punctual in attendance

   _____

5. acted without provocation
   A stirring someone to anger
   B a cause of annoyance

   _____

Name _____ Date _____

Writing

Suppose you have just read about the discovery of a sunken ship. You want to join the search team that will try to find lost treasures.

Write a letter to the person in charge of the search. Convince him or her that you should be chosen for the team. Use some vocabulary words from this unit in your writing.

_____
(Date)

To whom it may concern:

    I would like to join your search team. _____

_____

_____

_____

_____

_____

_____

_____

_____

_____

_____

Tarahumara Racers

Read the passage below. Think about the meanings of the **boldfaced** words.

It is race day for the Tarahumara Indians. Their aim is to run a 90-mile race. It will not be easy to meet their **goal**. They must run over a **rugged** mountain course. There are sharp rocks and uneven ground. They will run the course without stopping. Some will even run without shoes. It takes great **determination** to run this race. Each runner needs a strong spirit. There are many hardships to **overcome**. The runners must rise above these difficulties.

The Tarahumara live in the mountains and deep valleys of northern Mexico. Their races are an important part of their lives. The races have been held for hundreds of years. Usually there are two races a year. They celebrate times of harvest in different parts of the country.

Teams of male runners from two villages run against each other. The **opponents** play a game as they run. Each one uses the top of a foot to scoop up a ball and throw it. The first player to send the ball over the finish line claims **victory** for his team. His team wins!

How do the runners keep from getting tired on the 15-hour races? Many of them tie deer hooves to their belts. They fight **weariness** by listening to the sound of the hooves beating together.

Loneliness is not a problem for the runners. There are always other people close by. They offer water to the strong and **hardy** runners. They also carry torches to help runners see at night. In these ways, other village members help the runners **endure** the many hardships of the race. The winners are proud of themselves. And so are the other members of the village.

Go back to the passage. Underline the words or sentences that give you a clue to the meaning of each **boldfaced** word.

Name _____ Date _____

Context Clues

Meanings for the vocabulary words are given below. Go back to the passage and read each sentence that has a vocabulary word. If you still cannot tell the meaning, look for clues in the sentences that come before and after the one with the vocabulary word. Write each word from the box in front of its meaning.

| goal | overcome | determination | rugged | hardy |
| opponents | loneliness | endure | victory | weariness |

1. _____: wanting to be with others
2. _____: an aim; something wished for
3. _____: put up with
4. _____: the will to go on and not quit
5. _____: people trying to win the same contest
6. _____: tough; able to stand harsh conditions
7. _____: the feeling of being very tired
8. _____: rough and bumpy
9. _____: success
10. _____: conquer; defeat

Challenge Yourself

1. Name two goals you have.

   _____

2. Name two places where you can find opponents.

   _____

Name _____   Date _____

Synonyms

Remember that **synonyms** are words that have the same or almost the same meaning. Cross out the word in each line that is not a synonym.

1. rugged   smooth   harsh   rough
2. hardy   strong   healthy   weak
3. endure   continue   end   last
4. overcome   fail   defeat   beat
5. goal   start   aim   purpose
6. victory   failure   win   success
7. opponents   challengers   competitors   teammates
8. weariness   strength   exhaustion   fatigue

Dictionary Skills

Write the words in alphabetical order, one word on each line. Then turn to the Glossary, beginning on page 108. Find each word and write its meaning below.

| loneliness | determination | weariness | goal |
| victory | opponents | overcome | hardy |

1. _____
2. _____
3. _____
4. _____
5. _____
6. _____
7. _____
8. _____

Name _____   Date _____

Analogies

Remember that an **analogy** shows how two words go together in the same way as two other words. Write the words from the box to complete the following analogies.

| opponents | loneliness | determination | victory | weariness |

1. *Friend* is to *enemy* as _____ is to *defeat*.
2. *Players* is to *game* as _____ is to *contest*.
3. *Answer* is to *reply* as _____ is to *courage*.
4. *Name* is to *title* as _____ is to *tiredness*.
5. *Hunger* is to *food* as _____ is to *friend*.

Writing Sentences

Use each vocabulary word in the box to write an original sentence.

| goal | rugged | opponents | victory | hardy |

1. _____
2. _____
3. _____
4. _____
5. _____

Name _____ Date _____

Crossword Puzzle

Use the clues and the words in the box to complete the crossword puzzle.

| goal | overcome | determination | rugged | hardy |
| opponents | loneliness | endure | victory | weariness |

Across
2. to get the better of
5. uneven
8. great willpower in doing something
10. people you are competing against in a contest

Down
1. being alone and wanting to be with others
3. worn-out feeling
4. able to put up with hard conditions
6. to put up with
7. a win
9. something wished for

Standardized Test Practice

Read each sentence carefully. Then choose the best answer to complete each sentence. Circle the letter for the answer you have chosen.

TIP Read carefully. Use the other words in the sentence to help you choose the missing word.

1. Her _____ is to get 100% on the test.
   - A school
   - B goal
   - C hardy
   - D better

2. The sharp rocks make this a _____ trail.
   - A endure
   - B happily
   - C rugged
   - D weariness

3. He will race against two _____.
   - A friend
   - B hardy
   - C trains
   - D opponents

4. Her _____ will not let her quit.
   - A shoes
   - B mother's
   - C determination
   - D overcome

5. A runner must be _____.
   - A grow
   - B strongly
   - C opponents
   - D hardy

6. A runner cannot give in to _____.
   - A weariness
   - B goal
   - C late
   - D lonely

7. Pain can be hard to _____.
   - A color
   - B endure
   - C smile
   - D loneliness

8. She must _____ her fear of animals to have a pet.
   - A victory
   - B rabbit
   - C overcome
   - D welcome

9. _____ makes her wish for company.
   - A Loneliness
   - B Apples
   - C Difficult
   - D Waited

10. A _____ makes a team happy!
    - A victory
    - B rugged
    - C defeat
    - D conquer

Name _____ Date _____

Explore Word Meanings

Read and respond to each of the following statements or questions. Use complete sentences. Consult the glossary or a dictionary if you need help.

1. Should a deepwater diver show *stamina* or *lethargy*? Explain your answer.

2. In weightlifting, what is more important, *sturdiness* or *endurance*? In cross-country running? Explain your answer.

3. If someone is feeling *lackadaisical* or *languid*, how might he or she act?

4. If you were training for a race, what might you do to increase your *stamina*?

5. What might cause someone to feel *lethargic*?

Name _____   Date _____

Synonyms/Antonyms

Words with nearly the same meaning are called **synonyms**. Replace each underlined word with a synonym from the box. Write the new sentences.

| drowsiness   stamina   vim |

1. I ran a little farther each day to build up my <u>endurance</u> before the marathon.

   _____

2. Everyone wants to be around Sally because she is full of <u>vitality</u>.

   _____

3. <u>Lethargy</u> is not uncommon after long trips.

   _____

Words that have the opposite meanings are called **antonyms**. Replace each underlined word with an antonym from the box to change the meaning of the sentence. Write the new sentences.

| sturdiness   discombobulated   energetic |

4. <u>Languid</u> people typically lead active lifestyles.

   _____

5. <u>Weakness</u> is an important physical characteristic of most football players.

   _____

6. After my friends spent the night, my room was completely <u>organized</u>.

   _____

Name _____   Date _____

Word Origins/Etymology

The English language has grown over the centuries by borrowing words from other languages. Read the words in the box. Then choose the best word to complete each of the sentences. Look for context clues in the sentences to help you choose the right word. Write the word on the line.

| ballot | chandelier | Fahrenheit | judo | patriotism |
| pilgrim | planet | ranch | stamina | umbrella |

1. The word _____ comes from a Latin word that means "threads of human life" or "vital capacities."

2. The word _____ comes from a Japanese word that means "gentle way." This method of fighting is not as rough as other Japanese ways of fighting.

3. The word _____ comes from an Italian word meaning "little ball." People would cast their votes by putting little balls into a voting box.

4. The word _____ comes from the name of a German scientist who devised this scale for measuring temperature.

5. The word _____ goes back to a Greek word meaning "wandering star."

6. The word _____ comes from a French word meaning "candlestick." Today, it refers to an elaborate lighting fixture that hangs from the ceiling.

7. _____ goes back to the Greek word for "native land."

8. The word _____ comes from a Latin word that means "foreigner" and was used to refer to someone who had traveled far from home.

9. The word _____ comes from a Spanish word that means "a camp" or "a small farm." Today, however, it is often a very large estate.

10. The word _____ comes from a Latin word meaning "shade" or "shadow."

Writing

The Tarahumara run together as a team. They help each other to achieve their goal of victory.

On the lines below, write about a time when you were part of a team. A team could be you and a friend, a group of friends, or even your family. How did you work together? What was your goal? Use some vocabulary words from this unit in your writing.

Icarus and Daedalus

from *Old Greek Folk Stories Told Anew* by Josephine Preston

Read the story. Think about the meanings of the **boldfaced** words.

In this ancient Greek legend, Daedalus and his son, Icarus, plan an escape from the island of Crete. What happens when Icarus does not listen to his father's warning about their daring flight?

Among all those **mortals** who grew so wise that they learned the secrets of the gods, none was more cunning than Daedalus.

He once built, for King Minos of Crete, a wonderful labyrinth of winding ways so cunningly tangled up and twisted around that, once inside, you could never find your way out again without a magic clue. But the king's favor **veered** with the wind, and one day he had his master architect **imprisoned** in a tower. Daedalus managed to escape from his cell; but it seemed impossible to leave the island, since every ship that came or went was well guarded by order of the king.

At length, watching the seagulls in the air—the only creatures that were sure of liberty—he thought of a plan for himself and his young son Icarus, who was **captive** with him.

Little by little, he gathered a store of feathers great and small. He fastened these together with thread, molded them in with wax, and so fashioned two great wings like those of a bird. When they were done, Daedalus fitted them to his own shoulders, and after one or two efforts, he found that by waving his arms he could winnow the air and cleave it, as a swimmer does the sea. He held himself aloft, wavered this way and that with the wind, and at last, like a great fledgling, he learned to fly.

Without delay, he fell to work on a pair of wings for the boy Icarus, and taught him carefully how to use them, bidding him beware of rash adventures among the stars. "Remember," said the father, "never to fly very low or very high, for the fogs about the earth would weigh you down, but the blaze of the sun will surely melt your feathers apart if you go too near."

For Icarus, these cautions went in one ear and out by the other. Who could remember to be careful when he was to fly for the first time? Are birds careful? Not they! And not an idea remained in the boy's head but the one joy of escape.

The day came, and the fair wind that was to set them free. The father bird put on his wings, and while the light urged them to be gone, he waited to see that all was well with Icarus, for the two could not fly hand in hand. Up they rose, the boy after his father.

At first there was a terror in the joy. The wide vacancy of the air dazed them—a glance downward made their brains **reel**. But when a great wind filled their wings, and Icarus felt himself **sustained**, like a halcyon bird in the hollow of a wave, like a child **uplifted** by his mother, he forgot everything in the world but joy. He forgot Crete and the other islands that he had passed over. He saw but **vaguely** that winged thing in the distance before him that was his father Daedalus. He longed for one **draft** of flight to quench the thirst of his captivity. He stretched out his arms to the sky and made towards the highest heavens.

Alas for him! Warmer and warmer grew the air. Those arms, that had seemed to uphold him, relaxed. His wings wavered, dropped. He fluttered his young hands vainly—he was falling—and in that terror he remembered. The heat of the sun had melted the wax from his wings; the feathers were falling, one by one, like snowflakes; and there was no one to help.

He fell like a leaf tossed down by the wind, down, down, with one cry that **overtook** Daedalus far away. When he returned, and sought high and low for the poor boy, he saw nothing but the bird-like feathers afloat on the water, and he knew that Icarus was drowned.

The nearest island he named Icaria, in memory of the child; but he, in heavy grief, went to the temple of Apollo in Sicily, and there he hung up his wings as an offering. Never again did he attempt to fly.

Go back to the story. Underline the words or sentences that give you a clue to the meaning of each **boldfaced** word.

Name _____ Date _____

Context Clues

Meanings for the vocabulary words are given below. Go back to the story and read each sentence that has a vocabulary word. If you still cannot tell the meaning, look for clues in the sentences that come before and after the one with the vocabulary word. Write each word from the box in front of its meaning.

| captive | draft | mortals | reel | overtook |
| imprisoned | vaguely | veered | sustained | uplifted |

1. _____: beings who must die; humans who do not have the power of the gods

2. _____: to spin; to become dizzy

3. _____: kept and held without permission

4. _____: caught up with

5. _____: a drink

6. _____: not clearly

7. _____: raised up

8. _____: changed or shifted direction

9. _____: locked up; put into a jail

10. _____: supported

Challenge Yourself

1. Name two kinds of mortals.

_____

2. Name two places to imprison someone.

_____

Name _____ Date _____

Synonyms

Synonyms are words that have the same or almost the same meaning. Read each underlined word on the left. Circle its synonym on the right.

1. captive   captain   held   happy
2. sustained   supported   released   flew
3. draft   trail   feather   drink
4. reel   actual   whirl   shock
5. veer   shift   address   escape
6. uplifted   dropped   raised   grown

Antonyms

Antonyms are words that have opposite meanings. Write a word from each box that is an antonym for the underlined word or phrase in each sentence.

| reel | imprisoned | vaguely |
| overtook | veered | mortals |

1. Could you see it clearly or _____?

2. The winner _____ the other runner, who fell back.

3. Instead of going straight, the cart's wheels _____ to the left.

4. For ten years they were _____, and then they were set free.

5. While the gods live forever, _____ on Earth do not.

6. The ride made my head _____, so it was nice to stand still.

Name _____   Date _____

Figurative Language

Figurative language is using words in a colorful way.

An **idiom** is an expression in which the words together take on a meaning that is slightly different from the one they usually have separately. For example, if someone orders more food than he can eat, he might say, "My eyes were bigger than my stomach."

A **simile** is a figure of speech that compares unlike things, often with the words *like* or *as*. An example of a simile is, "She runs like a deer."

A **metaphor** is also a figure of speech that compares two things but without using *like* or *as*. An example of a metaphor is, "The wind is a knife through my jacket."

Complete this idiom from the story. Then explain what the expression means.

1. "For Icarus, these cautions went in one ear and _____."

2. _____

Complete this simile from the story. Then find and write another simile that compares Icarus to something.

3. "The heat of the sun had melted the wax from his wings; the feathers were falling, one by one, like _____; and there was no one to help."

4. _____

Write your own metaphor about Icarus or Daedalus.

5. _____

Name _____   Date _____

Standardized Test Practice

Read each sentence. Pick the word that best completes the sentence. Circle the letter for that word.

> **TIP**
> Be sure to find the letter of the answer you think is correct and then circle the letter.

1. The wild animal was _____ in a cage.
   - **A** reeled
   - **B** vaguely
   - **C** veered
   - **D** imprisoned

2. _____ don't have the powers of the gods.
   - **A** Mortals
   - **B** Drafts
   - **C** Sustained
   - **D** Reels

3. I _____ off the bike path to avoid hitting a squirrel.
   - **A** captive
   - **B** veered
   - **C** overtook
   - **D** current

4. The queen was held _____ in the tower.
   - **A** mortals
   - **B** softly
   - **C** vaguely
   - **D** captive

5. The bird was _____ in the air by its wings.
   - **A** sustained
   - **B** sunk
   - **C** draft
   - **D** vaguely

6. A _____ of water was all the thirsty hiker wanted.
   - **A** captive
   - **B** reel
   - **C** draft
   - **D** sustained

7. The baby princess was _____ and shown to the crowd below.
   - **A** mortals
   - **B** draft
   - **C** uplifted
   - **D** veered

8. I _____ remember seeing that show long ago.
   - **A** draft
   - **B** regret
   - **C** peacefully
   - **D** vaguely

9. The fast ride made our heads _____.
   - **A** daze
   - **B** reel
   - **C** mortals
   - **D** captive

10. The speeding car soon _____ the slow truck.
    - **A** overtook
    - **B** frequent
    - **C** uplifted
    - **D** draft

Vocabulary in Context

Name _____   Date _____

Rhyming Words

Translate the sentences below into rhyme by writing one word from each box. Then underline the words or phrases in the sentence that gave you the clue to the answer. Use the glossary or a dictionary if you need help with word meaning.

intrepid	chivalrous	lionhearted
valiant	doubtless	talent

elephant	gallant	tepid
omnivorous	departed	dauntless

Example: The <u>noble</u> knight <u>ate meat, grains, fruit and vegetables.</u>

The knight was _____*chivalrous*_____ and _____*omnivorous*_____.

1. After a few minutes, the courageous man left the scene.

   The _____ man soon _____.

2. The one thing that Sir Sneed was very good at was being brave and noble.

   Sir Sneed had a _____ for being _____.

3. There is no doubt that he is fearless.

   It's _____ that he's _____.

4. Marcus was brave and bold. He would swim across the river. He was glad the water was lukewarm.

   Marcus was _____, and the water was _____.

5. The large gray mammal bravely defended her calf from the hungry lions.

   She was a _____ _____.

Name _____ Date _____

Using Synonyms

Write the word(s) from the box that are synonyms for the words below. Use each word only once.

| chivalrous | dauntless | lionhearted | valiant |
| indomitable | gallant | mettlesome | intrepid |

1. noble, knightly, _____

2. unconquerable, unbeatable, _____

3. high-spirited, _____

4. bold, brave, fearless, _____

Now write an adjective from the box above to complete each phrase. More than one word might work.

5. the _____ knight

6. the _____ king (or ruler)

7. the _____ animal trainer

8. the _____ explorer

9. the _____ astronaut

10. the _____ firefighter

11. the _____ athlete

12. the _____ soldier

Name _____ Date _____

Confusing Words

The following pairs of words can be easily confused. Read the definitions. Then write the word from the pair that matches each definition.

mettlesome **meddlesome**

1. tending to interfere in other people's business _____

2. being full of vigor and having a strong spirit _____

indomitable **abominable**

3. stubbornly persistent; unconquerable _____

4. very disagreeable or unpleasant _____

gallant **gallon**

5. chivalrous or brave _____

6. a unit of liquid measure _____

valiant **valance**

7. a short drapery that covers the top of curtains _____

8. acting with bravery, boldness, or courage _____

chivalry **shivery**

9. qualities worthy of a knight or gentleman _____

10. trembling from cold or fear _____

Name _____ Date _____

Writing

Pretend that you have been asked to write a science fiction story for a magazine telling about your ability to fly. Think about words that describe how you feel as you fly up, up, and away.

On the lines below, describe your flight. How did it feel? Where did you go? Use some vocabulary words from this unit in your writing.

_____

_____

_____

_____

_____

_____

_____

_____

_____

_____

_____

_____

Walking in Space

Read the passage below. Think about the meanings of the **boldfaced** words.

In February 1995, six **dedicated** astronauts sat aboard the space shuttle *Discovery*. They would live there for the next eight days. "Four, three, two, one, **liftoff**!" The space shuttle rose into space.

Dr. Bernard Harris, Jr., was among the six loyal men crowded into the shuttle's **capsule**. He knew that the flight would put his name in the history books. He would be the first African American to walk in space.

Astronauts go through many months of training. They learn to follow their leader's directions. They also learn to act quickly when their **commander** gives an order. Each person's **assignment** changes from time to time. Learning to do different kinds of work means that each person can do the work of another crew member if needed. All crew members are taught how to use the controls in the **cockpit**. They are also **instructed** in other ways of working in that part of the capsule.

The hardest part of the training is getting used to being weightless. On Earth, the **gravitational** pull of the planet gives us weight. In space, the pull of Earth on our bodies becomes very weak. So astronauts in space are weightless. They float like balloons in the air.

One way that astronauts become used to the **sensation** of weightlessness is by flying in special planes. The planes climb fast and come down fast. The astronauts feel weightless for a few minutes. The planes do this **aerial** trick over and over. Slowly the riders get used to the feeling of floating in space. This training proved useful. Harris and astronaut Michael Foale walked—and floated—in space for five hours!

Go back to the passage. Underline the words or sentences that give you a clue to the meaning of each **boldfaced** word.

Name _____ Date _____

Context Clues

Read each sentence. Write a word from the box to complete each sentence.

| assignment | capsule | aerial | gravitational | dedicated |
| cockpit | commander | sensation | instructed | liftoff |

1. Dr. Bernard Harris, Jr., is a _____ astronaut who has spent many years in America's space program.

2. Dr. Harris was _____ by great teachers.

3. In 1995, his flight _____ was to ride in the space _____ on the shuttle *Discovery*.

4. At the end of the countdown, *Discovery* was ready for _____.

5. The _____ gave orders to the crew.

6. In space, there is no _____ pull, so a person feels weightless.

7. Being weightless is a strange _____.

8. The *Discovery* crew steered the spaceship from the _____.

9. From space, the astronauts had a beautiful _____ view of Earth.

Challenge Yourself

1. Name two things you might see in an aerial view of Earth.

   _____

2. Give two examples of a work assignment you have had.

   _____

Name _____ Date _____

Word Sense

Read each phrase. Check the glossary to see if the words make sense together. If they do, write *yes* on the line. If they do not, write *no* on the line and think of a word that does make sense with the underlined word. Write your word and the underlined word on the line.

1. gravitational <u>boy</u> _____
2. teacher <u>instructed</u> _____
3. confident <u>commander</u> _____
4. dedicated <u>sandwich</u> _____
5. purple <u>sensation</u> _____
6. difficult <u>assignment</u> _____
7. smiling <u>capsule</u> _____
8. smooth <u>liftoff</u> _____
9. curious <u>cockpit</u> _____
10. <u>aerial</u> book _____

Synonyms

Remember that **synonyms** are words that have the same or almost the same meaning. Read each underlined word on the left. Circle its synonym on the right.

1. <u>dedicated</u>   worried   devoted   finished
2. <u>sensation</u>   feeling   size   attitude
3. <u>commander</u>   building   chief   robot
4. <u>instructed</u>   promised   taught   related
5. <u>assignment</u>   help   pleasure   job

Crossword Puzzle

Use the clues and the words in the box to complete the crossword puzzle.

capsule	dedicated	cockpit	assignment	aerial
instructed	sensation	gravitational	liftoff	commander

Across
4. related to gravity
7. loyal
8. leader
9. enclosed part of a spacecraft
10. area where a pilot works

Down
1. the act of leaving the ground
2. taught
3. feeling
5. job to be carried out
6. in the air

Name _____ Date _____

Related Words

Read each sentence. Find a word in the sentence that is related to one of the words in the box. Underline the word in the sentence. Then write the word from the box on the line.

dedicated	assignment	sensation
commander	gravitational	instructed

1. The shuttle is under the command of one man. _____

2. He will assign specific tasks to each person. _____

3. The astronauts will study the effects of gravity. _____

4. They will follow precise instructions. _____

5. Their dedication to their work is remarkable. _____

6. What a sense of pride they give us! _____

Writing Sentences

Use each vocabulary word in the box to write an original sentence.

| capsule | liftoff | aerial | cockpit |

1. _____
2. _____
3. _____
4. _____

Standardized Test Practice

Read the sentences. Look for the best word to complete each sentence. Circle the letter for your choice.

TIP Read carefully. Use the other words in the sentences to help you choose the missing word.

1. The engines were fired. The spacecraft was ready for _____.
   A assignment   C liftoff
   B capsule   D messengers

2. The astronauts put on safety straps. They sat in the _____.
   A capsule   C kitchen
   B commander   D arena

3. Matt read about space. He did this for a class _____.
   A assignment   C sensation
   B capsule   D liftoff

4. The film provided information about space travel. It _____ the astronauts about flight.
   A remembered   C instructed
   B dedicated   D scolded

5. Anne told crew members what to do. She was the spacecraft _____.
   A assignment   C capsule
   B commander   D student

6. The astronauts flew safely. They controlled the shuttle from the _____.
   A commander   C liftoff
   B cockpit   D wings

7. People float in space. This happens because there is no _____ pull.
   A early   C dedicated
   B aerial   D gravitational

8. The pictures of Earth were taken from the sky. They were _____ photographs.
   A narrow   C sensation
   B aerial   D assignment

9. The astronauts spent years in training. They were _____ to their work.
   A miserable   C dedicated
   B new   D aerial

Name _____   Date _____

Greek Roots

Aero is a Greek root meaning "air." Match each word in the first column with the appropriate definition from the second column. Write the correct letter on the line.

1. _____ aerobics
2. _____ aerodynamic
3. _____ aeronautic
4. _____ aerosol
5. _____ aerospace

A. concerning the flight of aircraft

B. dispensing liquid through a valve in the form of a spray

C. to do with the forces exerted by air or motion

D. Earth's atmosphere and beyond

E. exercises that increase the body's ability to take in and use oxygen

Use what you know about words and word parts to define the following words. Then write a sentence using each.

6. aerial _____
_____

7. aerobatics _____
_____

Compare and Contrast

The first word in each sentence below contains a word formed with a Greek root. Use your knowledge of the words or use the glossary to complete each sentence.

1. *Acrobatics* is like *gymnastics* except that _____
_____.

2. *Calisthenics* is like *ballet* because _____
_____.

3. *Asteroids* are like *meteoroids* except that _____
_____.

Name _____   Date _____

Using Related Words

Words may be related by meaning or by structure. Tell how each group of terms is related. Then add another word that belongs in the group.

1. acrobatics   gymnastics   calisthenics
   _____

2. aerosol   aerobics   aerodynamic
   _____

3. aeronautic   astronaut   nautical
   _____

4. aerospace   spacesuit   outer space
   _____

5. gymnastics   gymnasium   gymnastically
   _____

6. heart   lungs   brain
   _____

7. running   cycling   swimming
   _____

8. breezy   calm   windy
   _____

9. basketball   badminton   volleyball
   _____

10. skateboard   rollerblades   scooter
    _____

Name _____   Date _____

Acronyms

An **acronym** is a word formed from the initial letters or syllables of other words. Read the names and phrases below and write the acronym on the line.

1. National Aeronautics and Space Administration _____

2. North Atlantic Treaty Organization _____

3. United Nations International Children's Education Fund _____

4. Public Broadcasting System _____

5. Organization of Petroleum Exporting Countries _____

6. Self-contained underwater breathing apparatus _____

7. Prisoner of war _____

8. Save our ship _____

Now try this. Match the phrases or names on the left with the acronyms on the right. Write the correct acronym on the line next to each phrase.

9. World Health Organization	_____	ASAP
10. Absent without leave	_____	HQ
11. As soon as possible	_____	ROM
12. Read-only memory	_____	AWOL
13. Zone Improvement Plan	_____	WHO
14. Random-access memory	_____	ZIP
15. Headquarters	_____	RAM

Name _____ Date _____

Writing

Imagine that you have the chance to fly on a space shuttle. Where would you like to go? What would you like to see? Remember that you would be weightless. How do you think it would feel?

On the lines below, tell about your spaceflight. What would you enjoy the most? What would you enjoy the least? Is there something special you would take with you? Use some vocabulary words from this unit in your writing.

_____
_____
_____
_____
_____
_____
_____
_____
_____
_____
_____
_____

Marvelous Jackie Robinson

Read the passage below. Think about the meanings of the **boldfaced** words.

Crack! Bat meets ball and the Dodgers' Jackie Robinson quickly runs to third base. But the players on the other team cannot tag him out. So he steals home, scoring a run. Robinson is also **superb** while playing second base. He is such an excellent **fielder** that he can catch even the most difficult balls. Jackie Robinson is truly amazing!

In 1947, Robinson was named Rookie of the Year. In 1949, he won more **recognition**. He received the National League's Most Valuable Player award. Each year his **popularity** grew. Other players and millions of fans admired him. But Robinson's popularity was based on more than just **athletic** skill. He was the first black to play Major League baseball.

Before Robinson, there had been an unwritten rule that blacks could not play Major League baseball. Branch Rickey, the Dodgers' president, hated this rule. He felt it was very unfair. The rule made a **barrier** that shut fine players out of the game. To knock down this wall, Rickey had to choose a very brave person. Jackie Robinson was the man he chose. Robinson was **courageous** enough to play a fine game even while hearing terrible insults. This required great determination and confidence.

Robinson knew about **prejudice**, about unfair treatment of blacks and others. He wanted **equality** for blacks so they would be treated the same as whites. With guts and skill, Robinson was able to change things. His **influence** opened Major League sports to everyone.

Go back to the passage. Underline the words or sentences that give you a clue to the meaning of each **boldfaced** word.

Name _____ Date _____

Context Clues

Meanings for the vocabulary words are given below. Go back to the passage and read each sentence that has a vocabulary word. If you still cannot tell the meaning, look for clues in the sentences that come before and after the one with the vocabulary word. Write each word from the box in front of its meaning.

prejudice	barrier	fielder	courageous	influence
equality	superb	athletic	recognition	popularity

1. _____: an effect on other people or things

2. _____: something that stands in the way

3. _____: condition of being the same

4. _____: brave

5. _____: excellent; splendid

6. _____: baseball player who plays around or outside the diamond

7. _____: state of being liked by others

8. _____: skilled at sport for which a person needs strength, ability, and speed

9. _____: attention

10. _____: opinion formed without knowing or caring about the facts

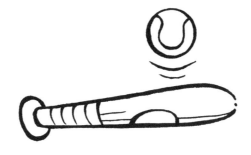

Name _____ Date _____

Related Words

Read each sentence. Find a word that is related to one of the words in the box. Underline the word in the sentence. Then write the word from the box on the line.

| recognition | athletic | popularity |
| courageous | equality | superb |

1. The story is about an athlete. _____

2. Did he recognize what lay ahead? _____

3. He was a popular player. _____

4. People admired his courage. _____

5. His skill was more than equal to that of other players. _____

6. He played baseball superbly. _____

Writing Sentences

Use each vocabulary word in the box to write an original sentence.

| influence fielder barrier prejudice |

1. _____

2. _____

3. _____

4. _____

Name _____ Date _____

Tangled-Up Words

A word is underlined in each sentence below. The word sounds similar to a word in the box. But its meaning makes it the wrong word for the sentence.

Read the paragraphs. Find the word in the box that should replace the underlined word. Write the vocabulary word on the line next to the number of the underlined word.

| recognition | equality | influence | barrier | fielder |
| athletic | superb | prejudice | courageous | popularity |

Jackie Robinson will be remembered for his (1) automatic ability. As a (2) feeler, he won many baseball awards. But his incredible (3) population comes from something else he did. He broke baseball's race (4) borrower. He believed that blacks and whites should have (5) quality. People admire what he did and say he was very (6) curious. He played a fine game in spite of terrible insults.

Jackie Robinson had an (7) endurance on baseball history. He was not only a (8) subway player. He spoke out against the (9) precious that kept him out of Major League baseball. His bravery and skill won him (10) permission forever. Fans will always remember marvelous Jackie Robinson.

1. _____
2. _____
3. _____
4. _____
5. _____
6. _____
7. _____
8. _____
9. _____
10. _____

Name _____ Date _____

Word Sense

Read each phrase. Check the glossary to see if the words make sense together. If they do, write *yes* on the line. If they do not, write *no* on the line and think of a word that does make sense with the underlined word. Write your word and the underlined word on the line.

1. given <u>recognition</u> _____
2. blue <u>popularity</u> _____
3. <u>superb</u> play _____
4. hat <u>fielder</u> _____
5. athletic <u>child</u> _____
6. jump <u>influence</u> _____
7. deserved <u>equality</u> _____
8. <u>courageous</u> tree _____
9. happy <u>barrier</u> _____
10. fair <u>prejudice</u> _____

Word Pairs

Words with similar parts may have related meanings. Study each word pair. Think about how the meanings of the words are alike. Check the meanings in the dictionary. Then write a sentence for each word.

1. super—superb

   _____

   _____

2. courage—courageous

   _____

   _____

Name _____ Date _____

Standardized Test Practice

Read the sentence or sentences. Look for the best word to complete the sentence. Circle the letter for your choice.

TIP
Be sure to mark the answer correctly. Do not mark the answer with an X or with a check mark. Instead, circle the letter neatly with your pencil.

1. She was an Olympic champion. She was _____ in field events.
   A superb   C courageous
   B prejudiced   D humorous

2. We all knew he worked hard for the award. He deserved our _____.
   A prejudice   C race
   B recognition   D barrier

3. Anyone can apply for the job. The company believes in _____.
   A influence   C limits
   B prejudice   D equality

4. He is the star of the team. He has strong _____ ability.
   A courageous   C recognition
   B shining   D athletic

5. The coach seems to show _____ by not letting girls play on the team.
   A promise   C prejudice
   B recognition   D equality

6. Everyone listens to what she says. Her _____ is strong.
   A influence   C fielder
   B barrier   D equality

7. They speak different languages. This creates a _____ between them.
   A recognition   C fielder
   B beginning   D barrier

8. Everyone likes Jan. Her _____ grows every year.
   A barrier   C equality
   B popularity   D doubt

9. The _____ lifeguard saved the drowning child.
   A hopeless   C prejudiced
   B courageous   D foolish

10. He caught the high fly ball. He's a great _____.
    A fielder   C climber
    B barrier   D superb

Vocabulary in Context

Name _____ Date _____

Synonyms and Antonyms

In each group, circle the two words that are **synonyms** for, or have a similar meaning to, the underlined word.

1. perspective	viewpoint	biased	outlook
2. ideology	events	ideas	beliefs
3. impartial	unbiased	fair	slanted
4. representation	likeness	politician	image
5. voice	hearing	opinion	point of view
6. flawed	imperfect	blemished	sensible
7. quilt	pillow	blanket	coverlet

Now circle the word or words that are **antonyms**, or opposites, of the underlined word.

8. biased	prejudiced	slanted	factual
9. comical	hilarious	serious	funny
10. complete	finished	unfinished	incomplete
11. partial	impartial	dangerous	burned
12. delicious	bland	scrumptious	tasteless
13. opinion	feeling	belief	fact
14. amateur	professional	beginner	athlete
15. demolish	build	destroy	establish

Name _____ Date _____

Multiple-Meaning Words

Some words have more than one meaning. Clues from the sentence tell you which meaning is being used. Read each sentence, paying attention to the underlined word. Circle the letter next to the correct meaning of the underlined word. Then use the other definition in a sentence.

1. A written passage that tells what the writer likes or dislikes reveals that writer's perspective.

   A the art of drawing an object on a flat surface so as to represent its three-dimensional look

   B a way of seeing things; a point of view

   _____

2. The writer's voice was evident in the descriptions of childhood scenes.

   A an individual's way of expressing himself or herself

   B the sound made by the vocal cords when speaking or singing

   _____

3. At the top of the hill, we stopped at an outlook so we could see the harbor.

   A a place from which you may view something

   B the way a person thinks or feels about something

   _____

4. At the town meeting, there was strong representation for the homeowners who were concerned about the new highway.

   A a depiction or portrayal, either visual or descriptive

   B the condition of having one or more persons acting on the behalf of others

   _____

5. Students are encouraged to record their reflections in a personal journal.

   A images given back by a shiny surface such as a mirror

   B ideas or statements that result from careful thought

   _____

Name _____   Date _____

Using Context Clues

For each sentence, use the context provided to write a definition of the underlined word.

1. I prefer to get facts from an impartial witness, preferably someone who does not know the people involved in the accident.

   _____

2. Mr. Thomas searched for a political candidate whose ideology he could agree with.

   _____

3. Advertisements are often biased because manufacturers tend to present only the advantages of owning their products.

   _____

4. I used to think that all dogs were mean, but my viewpoint has changed now that I have my own puppy.

   _____

5. The painter used perspective to show that the trees were quite far from the house and were not just very small.

   _____

6. This model is a good representation of the actual building.

   _____

7. The writer's voice showed clearly how she felt about the turtles.

   _____

8. His cheerful outlook raises the spirits of those around him even in hard times.

   _____

Writing

Jackie Robinson was a talented athlete. Yet for years he couldn't play Major League baseball because he was black. Do you know someone or know about someone who has been treated unfairly?

Write a paragraph about what happened to that person. Tell how you felt about it. Use some vocabulary words from this unit in your writing.

A Well-Ordered World

Read the passage below. Think about the meanings of the **boldfaced** words.

You're walking up a hill and stop to catch your breath. You look down and see ants scurrying in all different directions. It looks as if the ants don't know what they are doing or where they are going. Yet, ants have a very well-ordered world.

Within the **organization** of an ant colony, each ant has a job to do. Each colony has thousands of worker ants and one or more queen ants. Worker ants build the nest, find food, and take care of young ants. Groups **cooperate** on many tasks. They hurry and **bustle** about to help one another complete the work. At the center of their lives is the queen.

People have admired the well-ordered world of ants. They have wished that humans would cooperate as well as ants. Thousands of ants are crowded together in a **teeming** nest. Yet, they never fight each other. They fight only when there is an outside **threat**. Then they **defend** the nest against attack.

The worker ants accept the **authority** of the queen. The queen has a special way of giving orders. Her body makes a chemical on her skin that worker ants lick. Ants seem to like its taste. It makes them act in certain ways. It gives them orders. They pass the chemical and its messages on to other ants.

Young ants also have a chemical that sends messages or orders to adult worker ants. The worker ants like the taste of this chemical, too. Their orders are to feed and groom the young ants. Workers never seem to tire of caring for them. Their **tireless** care makes sure that the young ants grow up to be healthy. When the young ants reach **adulthood**, they become, in turn, worker ants.

The nest's **existence** depends on workers caring for the queen and the young ants. Nature programs ants to do particular kinds of jobs, and this makes for their well-ordered world.

Go back to the passage. Underline the words or sentences that give you a clue to the meaning of each **boldfaced** word.

Name _____ Date _____

Context Clues

Meanings for the vocabulary words are given below. Go back to the passage and read each sentence that has a vocabulary word. If you still cannot tell the meaning, look for clues in the sentences that come before and after the one with the vocabulary word. Write each word from the box in front of its meaning.

| cooperate | tireless | teeming | authority | organization |
| defend | threat | existence | adulthood | bustle |

1. _____: group that has a common purpose
2. _____: condition of being grown up
3. _____: to be noisy and busy
4. _____: full of life; swarming
5. _____: not needing rest
6. _____: to work together
7. _____: a state of being
8. _____: power to command
9. _____: something likely to cause harm
10. _____: to keep safe; protect

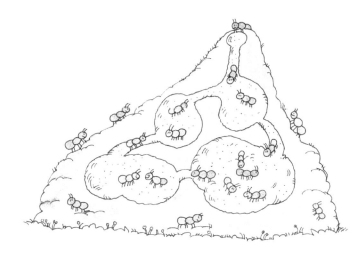

Name _____ Date _____

Writing Sentences

Use each word in the box to write an original sentence.

| existence | adulthood | tireless | organization |

1. _____
2. _____
3. _____
4. _____

Cloze Paragraphs

Use the words in the box to complete the paragraphs. Read the paragraphs again to be sure they make sense.

| threat | bustle | cooperate |
| authority | teeming | defend |

Can ants (1) _____ themselves successfully? When another insect or other animal becomes a (2) _____ to a fire ant, the fire ant stings. Other kinds of ants also refuse to (3) _____ with their enemies. They bite or spray a liquid to discourage the enemy from moving any closer.

Most ant colonies are (4) _____ with worker ants. They (5) _____ around their colony and work rather than fight. From whom do they get their orders? The queen has complete (6) _____.

Name _____ Date _____

Word Map

Use the vocabulary words in the box to complete the word map about ant colonies. Add other words that you know to each group.

| tireless | defend | bustle |
| organization | cooperate | authority |

1. Jobs of Worker Ants

_____
_____
_____
_____

2. Ways Ants Act

_____
_____
_____
_____

ANT COLONY

3. About the Ant Colony Queen

_____
_____
_____
_____

Name _____ Date _____

Word Sense

Read each phrase. Check the glossary to see if the words make sense together. If they do, write *yes* on the line. If they do not, write *no* on the line and think of a word that does make sense with the underlined word. Write your word and the underlined word on the line.

1. <u>cooperate</u> separately _____
2. peaceful <u>existence</u> _____
3. <u>teeming</u> paper _____
4. bravely <u>defend</u> _____
5. <u>bustle</u> quietly _____
6. <u>tireless</u> rug _____
7. happy <u>threat</u> _____
8. busy <u>adulthood</u> _____

Challenge Yourself

1. Name two <u>organizations</u> you belong to or know something about.

   _____

2. Name two people of <u>authority</u> that you know.

   _____

3. Name two ways you <u>cooperate</u> with students at your school.

   _____

Standardized Test Practice

Read each sentence. Pick the word that best completes the sentence. Circle the letter for that word.

> **TIP**
> Before you choose your answer, try reading the sentence with each answer choice. This will help you choose the answer that makes sense.

1. The teenager looked forward to _____.
   - **A** confusing
   - **B** threat
   - **C** adulthood
   - **D** yesterday

2. The _____ workers finished the job overnight.
   - **A** cooperate
   - **B** tireless
   - **C** about
   - **D** expand

3. The bees _____ about from flower to flower.
   - **A** commander
   - **B** bustle
   - **C** defend
   - **D** sky

4. A _____ crowd cheered the players.
   - **A** quickly
   - **B** silent
   - **C** defend
   - **D** teeming

5. We will _____ to get the job done.
   - **A** cooperate
   - **B** waste
   - **C** lamb
   - **D** authority

6. His _____ frightened us.
   - **A** tireless
   - **B** friendly
   - **C** threat
   - **D** vaguely

7. Our principal has the _____ to make rules.
   - **A** existence
   - **B** polite
   - **C** authority
   - **D** newspaper

8. It's fun to be a member of a good _____.
   - **A** organization
   - **B** existence
   - **C** teeming
   - **D** positive

9. Can you _____ your opinion?
   - **A** taste
   - **B** defend
   - **C** lifelike
   - **D** cooperate

10. The ant colony's _____ depends on the queen.
    - **A** tireless
    - **B** without
    - **C** flipper
    - **D** existence

Name _____ Date _____

Word Endings

When the word ending *-ing* is added to some verbs, the verbs become adjectives. Read the words below. Add the ending *-ing* to change the word from a verb to an adjective. Write the new word on the line. (Hint: Additional spelling changes will be needed for some words.)

1. fascinate _____
2. patronize _____
3. continue _____
4. restrain _____
5. dazzle _____
6. inspire _____
7. astonish _____
8. attract _____
9. overwhelm _____
10. accelerate _____
11. compel _____
12. recuperate _____
13. nauseate _____
14. beguile _____
15. captivate _____
16. charm _____

Using the words that you wrote above, decide which word fits best in each phrase below. Write the correct word on the line. Use the glossary or a dictionary if you need help with word meaning.

17. _____ rate of speed

18. _____ odor

19. _____ smile

20. a brave soldier's _____ story

21. _____ mystery story

22. a magician's _____ tricks

23. _____ patient in the hospital

24. the play's _____ performances

25. a magnet's _____ force

Name _____ Date _____

Using Context Clues

Read each of the following sentences, paying attention to the underlined words. Then write a definition for each underlined word.

1. The sweet-smelling flowers are teeming with bees in the garden.

   Teeming means _____.

2. The charming hostess delighted her guests with her kindness and wit.

   Charming means _____.

3. My new book was so fascinating that I could not put it down.

   Fascinating means _____.

4. The surprise party was astonishing because I wasn't expecting it.

   Astonishing means _____.

5. The student's story about volunteering and helping others was very inspiring.

   Inspiring means _____.

6. The playful puppy's cute tricks were beguiling to the children.

   Beguiling means _____.

7. The captivating actress thrilled the audience with her outstanding performance.

   Captivating means _____.

8. The movie was so compelling I couldn't take my eyes off the screen.

   Compelling means _____.

9. The dazzling sunshine hurt my eyes.

   Dazzling means _____.

10. The applause was overwhelming, and it made the actor cry.

    Overwhelming means _____.

Antonyms

Read the following sets of words. Find the pair of antonyms in each row and circle the two words.

1. talkative — useless — fascinating — ordinary
2. observe — recall — forget — view
3. attracting — repelling — movable — address
4. normal — create — brief — lengthy
5. sturdy — intelligent — enormous — fragile
6. astonishing — expected — positive — certain
7. confuse — energy — decline — accept
8. frisky — lazy — alert — wise
9. frozen — local — spoil — distant
10. athlete — amateur — professional — participate
11. ask — request — problem — solution
12. compelling — stylish — boring — garment
13. shallow — shaky — firm — unkind
14. captivating — dull — stretched — waterproof
15. support — knowledge — anxiety — confidence

Writing

Science-fiction writers often set their stories in other worlds. Begin a science-fiction story. Imagine that you have become small enough to visit the world of an ant colony. You explore the rooms and watch the ants' activities.

Write your story about what you see and do. Describe what happens to you. Use some vocabulary words from this unit in your writing.

Down, down, and down I went into the ant colony. _____

_____

_____

_____

_____

_____

_____

_____

_____

_____

_____

_____

Insect Self-Defense

Read the passage below. Think about the meanings of the **boldfaced** words.

Many insects end their short lives as the **victims** of other animals. Birds and fish hunt insects. Frogs, snakes, spiders, and bats **devour** them by the millions. Insects, of course, do not want to be eaten alive. So nature has given them a number of ways to stay away from their enemies.

Small insects often **conceal** themselves for safety. During the day, they hide in dark, secret places. At night, they come out to eat. This **behavior**, or way of acting, makes it less likely that enemies will spot them.

Other insects can hide right out in the open. Some moths, for example, are colored just like tree bark. Stick-insects look like twigs. Leaf-insects are flat and green. As long as these insects do not move, they are hard to find in nature. Once they move, however, they may **attract** an enemy.

Bees do not need to hide. They **specialize** in attacking their enemies. A small animal can be **paralyzed**, or made unable to move, by a bee sting.

Some insects are **poisonous**. Birds that eat and **digest** such insects become sick. So they learn to become more **attentive** to what they eat. They know which insects to avoid.

Insects have many ways of defending themselves in nature. They know how to hide so their enemies do not see them. They can attack or paralyze their enemies. They can even change their bodies to be less attractive to their enemies. But the most important way of protecting themselves is by having many offspring. Insects multiply by the millions. So, no matter how many are eaten, their numbers remain about the same.

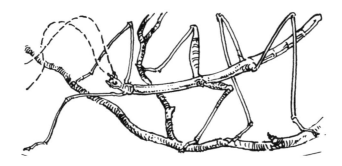

Go back to the passage. Underline the words or sentences that give you a clue to the meaning of each **boldfaced** word.

Context Clues

Meanings for the vocabulary words are given below. Go back to the passage and read each sentence that has a vocabulary word. If you still cannot tell the meaning, look for clues in the sentences that come before and after the one with the vocabulary word. Write each word from the box in front of its meaning.

| victims | behavior | paralyzed | digest | devour |
| specialize | poisonous | attentive | conceal | attract |

1. _____: a way of acting
2. _____: to be involved in one branch of work
3. _____: animals or people hurt or destroyed
4. _____: to eat hungrily
5. _____: to hide
6. _____: to gain attention
7. _____: containing harmful poison
8. _____: to change food in the body for the use of the body
9. _____: unable to move or feel
10. _____: alert; aware of

Name _____ Date _____

Word Groups

Read each pair of words. Think about how they are alike. Write the word from the box that best completes each group.

devour	paralyzed	poisonous	attract
attentive	specialize	behavior	conceal

1. harmful, deadly, _____

2. eat, taste, _____

3. hide, cover, _____

4. actions, manner, _____

5. watchful, alert, _____

6. frozen, motionless, _____

7. invite, lure, _____

8. focus, concentrate, _____

Challenge Yourself

1. Name two plants or animals that can be poisonous.

   _____

2. Name two foods you like to devour.

   _____

3. Name two places you can conceal yourself when playing hide-and-seek inside your home.

   _____

Name _____ Date _____

Word Sense

Read each phrase. Check the glossary to see if the words make sense together. If they do, write *yes* on the line. If they do not, write *no* on the line and think of a word that does make sense with the underlined word. Write your word and the underlined word on the line.

1. digest table _____
2. busy victims _____
3. specialize in medicine _____
4. attract attention _____
5. paralyzed laugh _____
6. attentive sleeper _____
7. poisonous spider _____
8. devour clothes _____
9. conceal a surprise _____
10. brown behavior _____

Word Pairs

Words with similar parts may have related meanings. Study each word pair. Think about how the meanings of the words are alike. Check the meanings in the dictionary. Then write a sentence for each word.

1. behave—behavior

   _____

   _____

2. attract—attraction

   _____

   _____

Name _____ Date _____

Dictionary Skills

Guide words are the two words at the top of each dictionary page. They show the first and last entries on that page. All the word entries in between are in alphabetical order. Look at the pairs of guide words. On the lines below each pair, write the words from the box that would appear on the same dictionary page. Be sure to put them in alphabetical order.

digest	paralyzed	behavior	victims	attentive
poisonous	specialize	devour	attract	conceal

1. artist/dip

2. pal/queen

3. rabbit/when

Now choose one word from each column. Write an original sentence using each word.

4. _____

5. _____

6. _____

Name _____   Date _____

Standardized Test Practice

Read the sentences. Look for the best word to complete each sentence. Circle the letter for your choice.

> **TIP**
> Read carefully. Use the other words in the sentences to help you choose the missing word.

1. Stay away from rattlesnakes. Their bite is _____.
   A happy   C harmless
   B full   D poisonous

2. The dog had not eaten for days. He began to _____ the food.
   A specialize   C write
   B devour   D give

3. I collect stamps from all over the world. However, I _____ in stamps from France.
   A think   C specialize
   B digest   D imagine

4. She always listens very carefully in class. She is very _____.
   A attentive   C poisonous
   B foolish   D lonely

5. Hide this present. I want to _____ it from my friend.
   A conceal   C borrow
   B attract   D divide

6. Cover the bowl. The sugar will _____ ants.
   A digest   C conceal
   B split   D attract

7. The boy could not move his legs after the accident. They were _____.
   A designed   C repeated
   B paralyzed   D attentive

8. Wolves run in packs. They run after and attack their _____.
   A behavior   C victims
   B voices   D driveways

9. Don't swim right after you eat. You need time to _____ your food.
   A specialize   C attract
   B digest   D entertain

10. The students were orderly during the fire drill. Their teachers were impressed with their _____.
    A childhood   C victims
    B handwriting   D behavior

Vocabulary in Context

Word Families

Words may be related by a root or base word, or by word parts, prefixes or suffixes. Use a dictionary or your knowledge to determine what the words in each group have in common. Then add another word that belongs to the same family. The first one has been done for you.

1. **A** carnage
   B carnivore
   C carnivorous
   Family: *root carn*
   Add: *carnival*

2. **A** herbal
   B herbivore
   C herbivorous
   Family: _____
   Add: _____

3. **A** omnivore
   B omnipresent
   C omnidirectional
   Family: _____
   Add: _____

4. **A** carnivore
   B voracious
   C herbivore
   Family: _____
   Add: _____

5. **A** rave
   B ravage
   C ravenous
   Family: _____
   Add: _____

6. **A** aquatic
   B aqueduct
   C aquarium
   Family: _____
   Add: _____

7. **A** astronomy
   B astronomer
   C astronomical
   Family: _____
   Add: _____

8. **A** biology
   B biography
   C biologist
   Family: _____
   Add: _____

9. **A** transatlantic
   B transcontinental
   C transport
   Family: _____
   Add: _____

10. **A** capable
    B agreeable
    C likable
    Family: _____
    Add: _____

Analogies

Analogies show how two pairs of words are related.

Fire is to *burn* as *wind* is to *blow*.

Complete the following analogies.

1. A *carnivore* is to *meat* as a *herbivore* is to _____.

2. *Ravenous* is to *eat* as *thirsty* is to _____.

3. *Carnivorous* is to *leopards* as *omnivorous* is to _____.

4. *Lions* are to *mammals* as *mosquitoes* are to _____.

5. *Similar* is to *different* as *compare* is to _____.

6. *Environment* is to *habitat* as *audience* is to _____.

7. *Protein* is to *muscles* as *calcium* is to _____.

8. A *geyser* is to *water* as a *volcano* is to _____.

9. *Cardiac* is to *heart* as *pulmonary* is to _____.

10. *Beginning* is to *end* as *initial* is to _____.

11. *Voracious* is to *hungry* as *exhausted* is to _____.

12. *Wet* is to *rain forest* as *dry* is to _____.

13. *Brush* is to *painter* as *pen* is to _____.

14. *Degree* is to *temperature* as *minute* is to _____.

15. *Agree* is to *disagree* as *give* is to _____.

Name _____ Date _____

Suffixes

Below are some suffixes and their meanings.

Suffix	Meaning	Suffix	Meaning
-ous	given to	-hood	state, condition
-ly	in a way that is	-er	one who
-en	made of	-ward	in the direction of

Read each sentence. Choose the correct suffix to add to the underlined word in parentheses. The words in parentheses are clues to help you decide which suffix should be used. Write the new word on the line. The first one is done for you.

1. The large _____*wooden*_____ table was loaded with platters of food. (made of wood)

2. My dog likes it when people _____ scratch her ears. (in a way that is gentle)

3. After the long journey, Simon was glad to be heading _____. (in the direction of home)

4. A tiger is an example of a _____ animal. (given to being a carnivore)

5. An elephant is an example of a _____ animal. (given to being a herbivore)

6. A human is an example of an _____ animal. (given to being an omnivore)

7. My parents often tell me that it is important to enjoy my _____. (state of being a child)

8. Who is your music _____? (one who teaches)

9. If you must talk when you're in the library, it is polite to talk _____. (in a way that is quiet)

10. The _____ coin was very rare and valuable. (made of gold)

Name _____ Date _____

Writing

Insects have different ways of defending themselves. Some, like bees, attack their enemies. Others, like praying mantises, have special ways of concealing themselves.

Write a paragraph discussing both types of insect defense. Which method do you think is more effective? Give reasons for your opinion. Use some vocabulary words from this unit in your writing.

Spiders Are Builders

Read the passage below. Think about the meanings of the **boldfaced** words.

You are trapped in a giant sticky net. A hairy monster appears and surrounds you. Its eight legs **encircle** you. This might sound like a bad dream to you. But it happens every night to millions of insects.

The monster is a spider, and the net is its web. To us, spider webs are **fragile**. But the webs are strong enough to hold most insects. Because the webs are **flexible**, they can bend to hold trapped insects in place.

A spider spins a web by letting out liquid silk from its body. The liquid dries and forms a thread. The spider ties one end of the silk to a wall or a tree. Then it **suspends** itself from the thread. As the spider hangs, the thread gets longer. A completed web might be made up of dozens of silk threads.

Spiders spin webs in many different shapes. The most common is **circular**, like a dinner plate. The web has threads that go from its center to its edges. The **diameter**, the distance across the web, may be as great as two feet.

Spiders also spin webs shaped like **rectangles**. These four-sided webs have **vertical** threads that run up and down. They also have **horizontal** threads running from side to side. These threads combine to form a kind of net. The net is used to catch insects for the spider to eat.

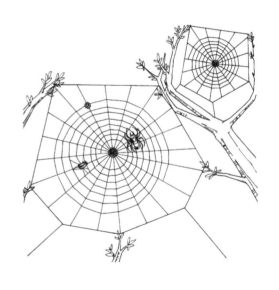

The web most people know is often seen in the corners of ceilings. These webs sometimes get tangled and collect dust. When that happens they are known as **cobwebs**. You are not likely to find a spider in a cobweb. A cobweb is not very useful. The spider cannot pull on the threads to catch insects. So it goes off to form another web, one that will help it get food.

Go back to the passage. Underline the words or sentences that give you a clue to the meaning of each **boldfaced** word.

Name _____ Date _____

Context Clues

Meanings for the vocabulary words are given below. Go back to the passage and read each sentence that has a vocabulary word. If you still cannot tell the meaning, look for clues in the sentences that come before and after the one with the vocabulary word. Write each word from the box in front of its meaning.

| fragile | circular | cobwebs | suspends | encircle |
| flexible | diameter | rectangles | vertical | horizontal |

1. _____ : in the same direction as the horizon
2. _____ : to form a circle around something
3. _____ : webs no longer used by spiders
4. _____ : easily destroyed
5. _____ : the distance from one side of a circle to another, passing through the center point
6. _____ : hangs
7. _____ : straight up and down
8. _____ : in the shape of a circle
9. _____ : four-sided shapes with four right angles and two sides that are longer than the other two
10. _____ : easily bent

Challenge Yourself

1. Name two things that are <u>fragile</u>.

_____

2. Name two things that you can <u>suspend</u> from the ceiling.

_____

Name _____ Date _____

Analogies

An **analogy** shows how two words go together in the same way as two other words. Write the words from the box to complete the following analogies.

suspends	fragile	circular
cobwebs	flexible	rectangles

1. *Steel* is to *strong* as *glass* is to _____.

2. *Buildings* are to *ruins* as *spider webs* are to _____.

3. *Balls* are to *circles* as *cartons* are to _____.

4. *Straight* is to *bent* as *stiff* is to _____.

5. *Four-sided* is to *square* as *round* is to _____.

6. *Leaps* is to *jumps* as *hangs* is to _____.

Writing Sentences

Use each vocabulary word in the box to write an original sentence.

encircle	suspends	vertical	fragile
diameter	horizontal	circular	flexible

1. _____
2. _____
3. _____
4. _____
5. _____
6. _____
7. _____
8. _____

Hidden Message Puzzle

Write a word from the box next to each clue. To find the message, copy the numbered letters in the matching numbered boxes at the bottom of the page. Then you will know why spiders play in the outfield.

> vertical rectangles encircle fragile
> flexible suspends cobwebs horizontal

1. to surround ☐☐☐☐☐☐☐☐
       1 11

2. straight up and down ☐☐☐☐☐☐☐☐
                  3

3. easy to bend ☐☐☐☐☐☐☐☐
       10   6

4. shapes with two long sides, two short sides, and right angles
☐☐☐☐☐☐☐☐☐☐
         12

5. unused webs ☐☐☐☐☐☐☐
        4

6. in the same direction as the horizon
☐☐☐☐☐☐☐☐☐☐
 5

7. hangs down while attached to something ☐☐☐☐☐☐☐☐
                          7   13

8. easily destroyed ☐☐☐☐☐☐☐
         9 2 8

ANSWER: Because they're good at

☐☐☐☐☐☐☐ ☐☐☐☐☐☐!
1 2 3 4 5 6 7 8 9 10 11 12 13

Name _____ Date _____

Yes or No?

Read each question. For a "yes" answer, write *yes* on the line. For a "no" answer, write a sentence that gives the correct meaning of the underlined word. Use the glossary or a dictionary if you need help.

1. Is a steel door <u>fragile</u>?

_____

2. If an object is <u>circular</u>, does it have corners?

_____

3. Can a dusty attic be filled with <u>cobwebs</u>?

_____

4. If the enemy is about to <u>encircle</u> your camp, are you in danger?

_____

5. If a tree has a <u>diameter</u> of three feet, is it a very young tree?

_____

6. If a circus act <u>suspends</u> the performer, is she on the ground?

_____

7. Does a <u>vertical</u> line zigzag?

_____

8. Are some televisions <u>rectangles</u>?

_____

9. Does a <u>flexible</u> material break easily?

_____

Name _____   Date _____

Standardized Test Practice

Read each phrase. Look for the word or words that have the same or almost the same meaning as the **boldfaced** word. Circle the letter for your choice.

Always read all the answer choices. Many choices may make sense. But only one answer choice has the same or almost the same meaning as the **boldfaced** word.

1. **suspends** a hammock
   A separates   C extends
   B hangs   D fixes

2. **encircles** the word
   A puts a circle around
   B takes a circle away
   C earns
   D repeats

3. **flexible** rim
   A fallen
   B easily attached
   C easy to bend
   D expected

4. **circular** driveway
   A in a flat shape
   B in a car's shape
   C in a long shape
   D in a circle shape

5. **fragile** vase
   A frightened   C enormous
   B delicate   D new

6. old **cobwebs**
   A spider webs   C corn silk
   B puzzles   D barns

7. **horizontal** line
   A curved
   B like the horizon
   C black
   D around Earth

8. **vertical** pole
   A up and down   C long
   B back and forth D valuable

9. measure the **diameter**
   A area of a room
   B list of ingredients
   C line around a square
   D line through a circle

10. wooden **rectangles**
    A shapes with three sides
    B apartments
    C shapes with four sides
    D sculptures

Name _____ Date _____

Content-Area Words

Each of the words in the box is used in the field of architecture. Write each word from the box next to its definition.

| Gothic | edifice | cornerstone | foundation |
| facade | gargoyle | architect | architecture |

1. the front of a building _____

2. the base of a building, which supports everything above it

   _____

3. a grotesque carved figure, such as an animal or a human, that contains a drain for rainwater _____

4. a stone that forms part of the corner of a building _____

5. a large and impressive building _____

6. a person who designs and plans buildings _____

7. a style of architecture used from AD 1200 to 1500 _____

8. the science or profession of designing buildings _____

Read and respond to each of the following questions.

9. What are some types of things an *architect* might design?

   _____

   _____

10. Why is the *foundation* the most important part of the building?

    _____

    _____

Name _____ Date _____

Related Words

Words may be related by meaning or by structural elements. Read each group of words and decide how the words are related. Then write a category name for each group.

1. facade, foundation, cornerstone   _____

2. tower, edifice, skyscraper   _____

3. architect, engineer, doctor   _____

4. sewing, weaving, knitting   _____

5. wood, bricks, cement   _____

6. Gothic, Baroque, Romanesque   _____

The groups of words below are related by base or root words. Cross out the word that is not related to the others and replace it with one that is. Write the new word on the line.

7. architect   architecturally   texture   architectural   _____

8. design   dessert   designed   designer   _____

9. bulletin   build   built   rebuilt   _____

10. construct   construction   conifer   reconstruct   _____

11. transfer   transport   tandem   transit   _____

12. create   credit   creative   creation   _____

Name _____ Date _____

Compare and Contrast

Complete the following sentences.

1. *Architecture* is like *sculpture* because _____
   _____.

2. A *skyscraper* is like an *edifice* because _____
   _____.

3. *Architecture* is like *construction* except _____
   _____.

4. A *gargoyle* is like a *statue* except _____
   _____.

5. *Gothic* is like *Baroque* because _____
   _____.

6. A *foundation* is like a *base* because _____
   _____.

7. A *blueprint* is like a *diagram* because _____
   _____.

8. A *facade* is like a *mask* because _____
   _____.

9. A *bridge* is like a *tunnel* because _____
   _____.

10. A *compass* is like a *map* because _____
    _____.

Name _____ Date _____

Writing

Spiders are not the only creatures that build their own homes. Bees build hives, and birds build nests. Men and women also build houses. Each home fits the needs of the person or animal that lives in it.

Compare a spider's home with another kind of home. Explain how they are alike and how they are different. Think about the shapes of the homes and the building materials used to create them. Also think about the purpose for each home. Use the information from the passage to help you. Use some vocabulary words from this unit in your writing.

_____
_____
_____
_____
_____
_____
_____
_____
_____
_____
_____
_____

Real Art?

Read the passage below. Think about the meanings of the **boldfaced** words.

For many years, people have written stories about robots, machines that can perform human actions. Sometimes these robots are strange beings from other planets in our solar system. Sometimes they come from other **galaxies**. Many Earth beings in the stories are eager to meet these **alien** beings from far away.

Sometimes the robots in stories are good. Sometimes they are not. Some story robots are clever **villains** who have fought to take over the world with their evil powers. They have **clashed** with the humans.

Almost every movie **version** of a robot story has been well liked by people who watch movies. To many movie **viewers**, the robots C3PO and R2D2 in the *Star Wars* movies are the real stars of the show. These good robots are **dependable**. They can be trusted. They are also eager to help the humans. They are not **ambitious** for power.

Make-believe robots are interesting. Today, though, they cannot hold more **fascination** than real robots. For example, one real robot is an artist. Meet AARON, a robot that paints pictures of people.

AARON is not a simple robot. He is an **elaborate** computer system developed over the last 30 years by artist Harold Cohen. Cohen wrote computer software to teach AARON to paint. AARON learned about drawing and painting and about the world. After many years of training, AARON can paint shapes and faces. His paintings can be seen in museums around the world. They are more popular than Cohen's own paintings.

For a long time, AARON painted what Cohen told him to paint. Now Cohen says that AARON decides what to paint. Can paintings created by a robot be real art? What do you think?

Go back to the passage. Underline the words or sentences that give you a clue to the meaning of each **boldfaced** word.

Name _____ Date _____

Context Clues

Meanings for the vocabulary words are given below. Go back to the passage and read each sentence that has a vocabulary word. If you still cannot tell the meaning, look for clues in the sentences that come before and after the one with the vocabulary word. Write each word from the box in front of its meaning.

dependable	villains	alien	ambitious	fascination
version	clashed	viewers	elaborate	galaxies

1. _____ : people who look at or watch something
2. _____ : one form of something
3. _____ : trustworthy
4. _____ : had a conflict; fought
5. _____ : from another planet; foreign
6. _____ : a strong interest or attraction
7. _____ : evil creatures
8. _____ : seeking something better
9. _____ : complicated
10. _____ : large groups of stars

Challenge Yourself

1. Name two places where you would find viewers.

_____

2. Name two characters in books or movies who are villains.

_____

Name _____   Date _____

Antonyms

Remember that **antonyms** are words that have opposite meanings. Write a word from the box that is an antonym for the underlined word in each sentence.

> elaborate   ambitious   alien
> dependable   fascination

1. She started with a <u>simple</u> plan that soon became very _____.

2. My cousin has a great _____ with mystery stories. For me, they bring on <u>boredom</u>.

3. She is _____, but her sister is <u>unreliable</u>.

4. Is the new worker _____, or is he <u>lazy</u> and uncaring?

5. The strange creature was certainly not a <u>native</u> one; it was an _____ being.

Rewriting Sentences

Rewrite each sentence using a vocabulary word from the box.

> dependable   villains   version   galaxies

1. I have always wanted to visit other groups of stars.

   _____

2. I would take along my trustworthy robot.

   _____

3. We would fight and conquer many evil creatures.

   _____

4. I could write a book and then make the movie form.

   _____

Name _____   Date _____

Related Words

Read each sentence. Find a word that is related to one of the words in the box. Underline the word in the sentence. Then write the word from the box on the line.

| fascination   viewers   ambitious   dependable   elaborate |

1. Art lovers are fascinated by the idea that paintings can be done by a robot.

   _____

2. Many people have gone to museums to view AARON's paintings.

   _____

3. AARON is an elaborately designed computer program.

   _____

4. AARON's ability to paint depends on the computer program.

   _____

5. Harold Cohen has achieved his ambition to create a robot artist.

   _____

Word Sense

Read each phrase. Check the glossary to see if the words make sense together. If they do, write *yes* on the line. If they do not, write *no* on the line and think of a word that does make sense with the underlined word. Write your word and the underlined word on the line.

1. distant <u>galaxies</u>   _____

2. kind <u>villains</u>   _____

3. ambitious <u>slippers</u>   _____

4. constant <u>fascination</u>   _____

Name _____ Date _____

Crossword Puzzle

Use the clues and the words in the box to complete the crossword puzzle.

| dependable | villains | alien | ambitious | fascination |
| version | clashed | viewers | elaborate | galaxies |

Across
4. complex; detailed
6. from another place
7. one kind
8. battled
9. wanting success

Down
1. groups of stars
2. reliable
3. the bad guys
5. strong appeal
7. those who watch

Standardized Test Practice

Read the sentences. Look for the best word to complete each sentence. Circle the letter for your choice.

TIP
If you are not sure which word completes the sentence, do the best you can. Try to choose the word that makes the most sense.

1. That is one of the most popular programs on TV. It has millions of ____.
   - **A** trainers
   - **B** viewers
   - **C** writers
   - **D** galaxies

2. Carol always arrives on time. She is very ____.
   - **A** expensive
   - **B** elaborate
   - **C** costly
   - **D** dependable

3. For months the thieves robbed stores. Finally, the police caught the ____.
   - **A** viewers
   - **B** villains
   - **C** galaxies
   - **D** gestures

4. He claimed that a spaceship landed. Out of the craft came ____ visitors.
   - **A** alien
   - **B** diamond
   - **C** loud
   - **D** furniture

5. The two had always been enemies. They ____ frequently.
   - **A** agreed
   - **B** helped
   - **C** clashed
   - **D** elaborated

6. Look at the stars through the telescope. You can see far-off ____.
   - **A** buildings
   - **B** mountains
   - **C** fascination
   - **D** galaxies

7. The cat could not take its eyes off the birds. It stared at them with ____.
   - **A** fascination
   - **B** glasses
   - **C** disgust
   - **D** bees

8. The necklace had beads of many colors and shapes. The design was ____.
   - **A** dependable
   - **B** plain
   - **C** red
   - **D** elaborate

9. I saw both the play and the film. I preferred the film ____.
   - **A** fascination
   - **B** light
   - **C** version
   - **D** boundary

10. Her goal was to make important discoveries in science. She was very ____.
    - **A** tired
    - **B** ambitious
    - **C** clashing
    - **D** dependable

Vocabulary in Context

Name _____ Date _____

Compare and Contrast

Read and complete each of the following statements.

1. *Handiwork* is like *handicraft* because _____
   _____.

2. *Handmade* is not like *manufactured* because _____
   _____.

3. *Artistry* is like *skill* except _____
   _____.

4. *Dexterity* is like *coordination* because _____
   _____.

5. *Expertise* is like *knowledge* except _____
   _____.

6. *Manipulate* is like *handle* because _____
   _____.

7. *Ability* is like *talent* because _____
   _____.

Now answer these questions.

8. What are some of your *abilities*? _____
   _____

9. What are some sports that require *dexterity*? _____
   _____

10. What are some examples of *handicrafts*? _____
    _____

Related Words

Words can be related by meaning or by word parts. Read each list of words and figure out the words' relationship to one another. Circle the letter of the word that does not fit and replace it with one that does.

1. A ability
    B talent
    C expertise
    D unskilled
    _____

2. A crafty
    B handicraft
    C handmade
    D handiwork
    _____

3. A manipulate
    B many
    C manifold
    D mania
    _____

4. A art
    B are
    C artist
    D artistry
    _____

5. A manipulate
    B maneuver
    C handle
    D avoid
    _____

6. A artistry
    B creativity
    C unimaginative
    D originality
    _____

7. A manufacture
    B expertise
    C make
    D produce
    _____

8. A pottery
    B sculpture
    C weaving
    D singing
    _____

9. A dexterity
    B skill
    C awkward
    D agility
    _____

10. A experience
    B exercise
    C expertise
    D expert
    _____

Name _____ Date _____

Classify/Categorize

Write each word from the box under the correct category. Then add two words of your own to each category.

> pottery   woodworking   machinery
> plastic containers   automobiles   needlepoint

1. Examples of Handicrafts

_____

_____

_____

_____

2. Things That Are Manufactured

_____

_____

_____

_____

Now try these.

> drawing   tennis   basketball
> golf   sculpting   painting

3. Sports That Require Dexterity

_____

_____

_____

_____

4. Activities That Require Artistry

_____

_____

_____

_____

5. Do artistic activities also require dexterity? Explain your answer.

_____

_____

Name _____ Date _____

Writing

Robots help build cars, assemble watches, and assist doctors. Think of some new tasks that robots could do to help people. Use your imagination!

On the lines below, tell about three jobs that robots could do for you. Tell why robots would be good for these jobs. Use some vocabulary words from this unit in your writing.

Glossary

A

ability	*noun*	power to do or perform (page 104)
acrobatics	*noun*	stunts performed by an acrobat; gymnastics (page 54)
adulthood	*noun*	the state of being fully grown up (page 68)
aerial	*adjective*	of or in the air (page 48)
aerobatics	*noun*	stunts done by an airplane, such as rolls or loops (page 54)
aerobics	*noun*	vigorous physical exercises to increase the use of oxygen (page 54)
aerodynamic	*adjective*	designed to work with the force of moving air (page 54)
aeronautic	*adjective*	having to do with designing, making, and flying aircraft (page 54)
aerosol	*noun*	a mass of extremely small particles suspended in a gas (page 54)
aerospace	*noun*	Earth's atmosphere and outer space, considered as a single region (page 54)
alien	*adjective*	from another planet (page 98)
amateur	*noun*	somebody doing something for pleasure, not for money (page 64)
ambitious	*adjective*	having a strong desire to do something; wishing for something better (page 98)
anthropologist	*noun*	a scientist who studies how people have lived together, from ancient times to the present (page 14)
archaeologist	*noun*	a scientist who studies the past by examining artifacts (page 8)
architect	*noun*	a person who designs and draws up plans for buildings (page 94)
architecture	*noun*	the science or profession of designing and putting up buildings (page 94)
artifacts	*noun*	items made by people long ago (page 8)
artistry	*noun*	artistic work or ability (page 104)

assignment	*noun*	job; the work someone is given to do (page 48)
asteroids	*noun*	small rocky objects that orbit the sun (page 54)
astonishing	*adjective*	amazing; surprising (page 74)
athletic	*adjective*	having to do with sports; good at sports and/or physically fit (page 58)
attentive	*adjective*	looking closely; paying careful attention (page 78)
attract	*verb*	to get the attention of; draw to oneself (page 78)
attracting	*adjective*	pulling; tempting (page 74)
authority	*noun*	the power to give orders (page 68)

B

Baroque	*adjective*	relating to a style of art and architecture developed in Europe from about 1550 to 1700 and characterized by complex forms (page 95)
barrier	*noun*	a wall; something that is in the way (page 58)
beguiling	*adjective*	charming; entertaining (page 74)
behavior	*noun*	way of acting (page 78)
biased	*adjective*	prejudiced; slanted (page 64)
billows	*noun*	large waves (page 18)
blueprint	*noun*	a print of a building plan (page 96)
botanist	*noun*	a scientist who studies plants (page 15)
buoy	*noun*	a float used as a warning or marker (page 18)
bustle	*verb*	to hurry in a noisy way (page 68)

C

calisthenics	*noun*	exercises done to promote health (page 54)
capsule	*noun*	the part of a spaceship that carries people (page 48)
captivating	*adjective*	fascinating, as by beauty or excellence (page 74)
captive	*adjective*	kept in a prison (page 38)
carnivore	*noun*	an animal that eats meat (pages 15 and 84)
carnivorous	*adjective*	eating or living on meat (page 84)
catalyst	*noun*	a substance that speeds up a chemical reaction (page 24)
chambers	*noun*	rooms (page 8)
charming	*adjective*	very attractive, pleasing, or delightful (page 74)

chivalrous	*adjective*	gallant and brave (page 44)
circular	*adjective*	round like a dinner plate (page 88)
civilization	*noun*	the society and culture of a people (page 8)
clashed	*verb*	fought; had a conflict (page 98)
cobwebs	*noun*	dusty, tangled spider webs (page 88)
cockpit	*noun*	the place where a pilot sits; the control center of a space shuttle (page 48)
commander	*noun*	the person who gives orders; the person in charge (page 48)
compelling	*adjective*	forceful; demanding (page 74)
conceal	*verb*	to hide (page 78)
cooperate	*verb*	to work together (page 68)
coordination	*noun*	skilled and organized movement of parts, such as muscles (page 104)
cornerstone	*noun*	a stone that forms part of the corner of a building (page 94)
courageous	*adjective*	very brave (page 58)
cunning	*adjective*	very clever; tricky (page 24)

D

dauntless	*adjective*	fearless; brave; daring (page 44)
dedicated	*adjective*	willing to work with great loyalty; devoted (page 48)
defend	*verb*	to keep safe; guard (page 68)
demolish	*verb*	to wreck; knock down (page 64)
dependable	*adjective*	able to be trusted (page 98)
destination	*noun*	the place to which something is going (page 18)
determination	*noun*	great willpower in doing something (page 28)
devour	*verb*	to eat (page 78)
dexterity	*noun*	skill in using the hands or body; agility (page 104)
diameter	*noun*	the distance across a circle (page 88)
digest	*verb*	to change food in the stomach into forms the body can use (page 78)
discombobulated	*adjective*	confused or upset (page 35)

discoverers	*noun*	people who find something (page 18)
draft	*noun*	a drink (page 39)
drowsiness	*noun*	sleepiness (page 35)

E

edifice	*noun*	a large and impressive building (page 94)
Egyptologist	*noun*	a person who studies ancient Egypt (page 14)
elaborate	*adjective*	complicated; having many parts (page 98)
encircle	*verb*	to go around; surround (page 88)
endurance	*noun*	the ability to keep going under hardship (page 34)
endure	*verb*	to put up with (page 28)
energetic	*adjective*	lively and active; full of energy (page 35)
equality	*noun*	the state of being equal, in which everyone is treated the same way (page 58)
evidence	*noun*	a sign that something is there or has happened (page 18)
evident	*adjective*	easy to see or tell; plain (page 8)
existence	*noun*	being (page 68)
expedition	*noun*	a journey with a special purpose (page 8)
expertise	*noun*	the special skill or knowledge of an expert (page 104)

F

facade	*noun*	the front of a building; an artificial front (page 94)
fascinating	*adjective*	extremely interesting (page 74)
fascination	*noun*	a strong attraction to something (page 98)
fielder	*noun*	a baseball player who tries to catch and throw balls hit into the field (page 58)
flexible	*adjective*	able to bend and not break (page 88)
flourish	*verb*	to grow and succeed (page 24)
foundation	*noun*	a base, as of a building, that supports everything above it (page 94)
fragile	*adjective*	not strong; weak; breakable (page 88)

G

galaxies	*noun*	large groups of stars (page 98)
gallant	*adjective*	bold and courageous (page 44)
gargoyle	*noun*	a carved figure that juts out from a building (page 94)
geologist	*noun*	a scientist who studies Earth's layers of rock and soil (page 15)
goad	*verb*	to drive or spur someone along (page 24)
goal	*noun*	something wished for; aim (page 28)
Gothic	*adjective*	relating to a style of architecture used in Europe from about 1200 to 1500 and characterized by pointed arches (page 94)
gravitational	*adjective*	having to do with gravity, or the force that pulls things toward Earth (page 48)
gymnastics	*noun*	exercises that require muscle control and strength (page 54)

H

handicraft	*noun*	skill in working with the hands; a trade, occupation, or craft requiring such skill (page 104)
handiwork	*noun*	work done by the hands; work done personally (page 104)
handmade	*adjective*	made by hand or by hand tools (page 104)
hardy	*adjective*	tough; able to put up with hard conditions (page 28)
herbivore	*noun*	an animal that feeds on plants (pages 15 and 84)
herbivorous	*adjective*	feeding on plants (page 84)
historian	*noun*	a writer or authority on history (page 15)
historic	*adjective*	very important; likely to be remembered for a long time (page 8)
horizontal	*adjective*	flat; going across (page 88)
hull	*noun*	the frame of a ship (page 18)

I

ideology	*noun*	the ideas or beliefs held by a class or group (page 64)

impartial	*adjective*	not favoring one thing or person (page 64)
imprisoned	*verb*	locked up; put in a prison (page 38)
incentive	*noun*	something that makes a person want to work or put forth effort (page 24)
indomitable	*adjective*	not easily defeated or overcome (page 45)
influence	*noun*	power over others (page 58)
inspiring	*adjective*	having the effect of filling with a desire to do something (page 74)
instructed	*verb*	showed how; taught (page 48)
intrepid	*adjective*	very brave; courageous; fearless (page 44)
investigate	*verb*	to look into with great care (page 8)

L

lackadaisical	*adjective*	without interest, energy, or concern (page 34)
languid	*adjective*	lacking energy or spirit; weak (page 34)
lethargy	*noun*	the condition of feeling tired, dull, and listless (page 34)
liftoff	*noun*	the act of rising from the ground and taking flight (page 48)
lionhearted	*adjective*	having great courage (page 44)
loneliness	*noun*	being alone and wanting to be with others (page 28)

M

manipulate	*verb*	to manage or control (page 104)
manufactured	*adjective*	made by machines (page 104)
meteoroids	*noun*	solid bodies, smaller than asteroids, moving in space (page 54)
mettlesome	*adjective*	full of spirit; courageous (page 45)
misanthrope	*noun*	a person who hates or distrusts other people (page 14)
mortals	*noun*	human beings (page 38)
motive	*noun*	a reason that makes a person act (page 24)

N

naturalist	*noun*	a person who studies objects in nature (page 15)

nauseating	*adjective*	disgusting (page 74)
nautical	*adjective*	relating to ships or sailors (page 55)
navigate	*verb*	to steer a boat or plane (page 18)

O

omnivore	*noun*	one that feeds on both animal and vegetable substances (page 84)
omnivorous	*adjective*	eating both animals and vegetables as food (page 44)
opponents	*noun*	people you are competing against in a contest (page 28)
organization	*noun*	a group of people working together for a specific purpose; an arrangement of parts to make a whole (page 68)
outlook	*noun*	the way a person thinks or feels about things (page 64)
overcome	*verb*	to get the better of; to win over (page 28)
overtook	*verb*	caught up with (page 39)

P

paralyzed	*verb*	made something unable to move (page 78)
perspective	*noun*	a way of seeing things in relation to one another; viewpoint (page 64)
philanthropist	*noun*	a person who devotes time and money to helping others (page 14)
poisonous	*adjective*	containing a substance that can cause sickness or death (page 78)
popularity	*noun*	being liked by many people (page 58)
prejudice	*noun*	unfair dislike of a group of people (page 58)
prod	*verb*	to urge someone or something (page 24)
prompt	*verb*	to urge or inspire (page 24)
provocation	*noun*	the act of making someone angry or resentful (page 24)
pyramids	*noun*	huge pointed buildings made of stone (page 8)

R

ravenous	*adjective*	wildly hungry (page 84)
recognition	*noun*	fame; attention given to someone who has done something good (page 58)
rectangles	*noun*	four-sided shapes with four right angles and two sides that are longer than the other two (page 88)
recuperating	*adjective*	regaining health; recovering (page 74)
reel	*verb*	to whirl; feel dizzy (page 39)
repelling	*verb*	keeping or forcing something away (page 76)
representation	*noun*	anything that stands for or describes something else, as a picture, a written description, or a symbol does (page 64)
robots	*noun*	machines that copy the actions of people (page 98)
rugged	*adjective*	rough; uneven (page 28)

S

scrumptious	*adjective*	delicious; delightful (page 64)
scuba	*adjective*	relating to equipment used for breathing underwater (page 18)
sensation	*noun*	feeling (page 48)
sociologist	*noun*	one whose job is to study people living in groups (page 14)
specialize	*verb*	to have a particular way of acting (page 78)
stamina	*noun*	strength; endurance (page 34)
stimulus	*noun*	anything that stirs to action or greater effort (page 24)
sturdiness	*noun*	the condition of being firmly built (page 34)
sunken	*adjective*	resting under the water (page 18)
superb	*adjective*	very good; excellent (page 58)
suspends	*verb*	hangs from something fastened above (page 88)
sustained	*adjective*	supported; held up (page 39)

T

teeming	*adjective*	full; crowded (page 68)
tepid	*adjective*	not hot or cold; lukewarm (page 44)

threat	*noun*	a sign of danger (page 68)
tireless	*adjective*	never becoming tired; never stopping (page 68)
tombs	*noun*	graves; places for dead bodies (page 8)

U

undersea	*adjective*	beneath the surface of the sea (page 18)
uplifted	*verb*	raised up and held in the air (page 39)

V

vaguely	*adverb*	in an unclear way; dimly (page 39)
valiant	*adjective*	having or showing courage; brave (page 44)
veered	*verb*	changed direction (page 38)
version	*noun*	one form of something (page 98)
vertical	*adjective*	in an up-and-down direction (page 88)
victims	*noun*	people or animals that are harmed or killed by another (page 78)
victory	*noun*	a win; success (page 28)
viewers	*noun*	people who look at or watch something (page 98)
viewpoint	*noun*	a position from which one looks at something (page 64)
villains	*noun*	wicked people (page 98)
vim	*noun*	energy; spirits (page 35)
vitality	*noun*	physical or mental strength and energy (page 35)
voice	*noun*	the expression of a thought in words; sound made through the mouth (page 64)
voracious	*adjective*	taking a great deal of something without getting enough (page 84)

W

weariness	*noun*	tiredness; worn-out feeling (page 28)

Answer Key

Page 9
1. archaeologists
2. civilization
3. expedition
4. pyramids
5. tombs
6. chambers
7. investigate
8. historic
9. artifacts
10. evident

Page 10
Word Groups
1. tomb
2. archaeologist
3. expedition

Cloze Paragraph
1. tomb
2. investigated
3. historic
4. civilization
5. artifacts
6. Archaeologists
7. evident
8. expedition

Page 11
Across
1. investigate
4. archaeologists
5. pyramids
6. tombs
7. chambers
8. civilization
9. historic

Down
2. evident
3. expedition

4. artifacts

Page 12
1. **ant/jump**
   archaeologists
   artifacts
   chambers
   civilization
   evident
   expedition
   historic
   investigate
2. **lemon/uneven**
   pyramids
   tombs
3.–4. Answers will vary.

Page 13
1. D
2. A
3. B
4. D
5. C
6. A
7. A
8. B
9. D
10. C

Page 14
1. a person who studies the physical, social, and cultural development of humans
2. a person who studies the past by examining artifacts
3. a person who does not like or trust others
4. a person who helps others
5. a person who studies groups or communities of people
6. Philadelphia contains the root *phil*, which means "love."
7. archaeology
8. the root *log* and the suffix *–ist*

Page 15
Answers may vary slightly.
1. Egyptologist
2. love

3. people
4. archaeologist
5. history
6. animals
7. numbers
8. battery
9. flock
10. square
11. feet
12. plants
13. liquid
14. yarn
15. country

Page 16
Answers may vary. Accept reasonable responses.
1. A philanthropist might donate money or do volunteer work.
2. An Egyptologist might study pyramids, tombs, mummies, and other artifacts.
3. Historians are important because their writings help people understand and learn from the past.
4. It's unlikely that a misanthrope would be a sociologist because sociologists study people and misanthropes dislike people.
5. An archaeologist probably wouldn't be interested in studying the Second World War because archaeologists study ancient civilizations.
6. Anthropologists and sociologists both study people.

Page 17
Answers will vary based on students' personal experiences.

Page 19
1. sunken
2. destination
3. navigate
4. hull
5. evidence
6. discoverers
7. buoy
8. undersea
9. billows
10. scuba

Page 20
Word Origins
1. navigate   3. evidence
2. hull   4. scuba

Cloze Paragraph
1. undersea   4. buoy
2. sunken   5. destination
3. billows   6. discoverers

Page 21
Additional answers will vary.
1. Who Finds Treasure: discoverers
2. Where Treasure Is Found: sunken, undersea
3. Things Used to Hunt Treasure: scuba, buoy
4. Kinds of Treasure Found: (possible answers) gold coins, jewels

Page 22
1. scuba
2. buoy
3. navigate
4. undersea
5. destination
6. sunken
7. discoverers
8. evidence
9. hull
10. billows

Page 23
1. B   6. B
2. A   7. C
3. C   8. A
4. D   9. D
5. B   10. B

Page 24
1. stimulus, incentive
2. motive, reason
3. prod, goad
4. catalyst, incentive
5. prompt, urge
6. provocation, incitation
7. needless, unnecessary
8. cunning, sly
9. magnificent, splendid
10. possess, own
11. tired, exhausted
12. disease, illness
13. precipitation, rain
14. piece, part
15. grow, flourish
16. strong, powerful
17. performer, dancer
18. ruin, destroy

Page 25
Latin Roots
Possible answers are given.
1. A person offers an incentive so that others will perform a certain action; in this way, he or she is "setting the tune" for others to follow.
2. An actor who has forgotten his or her lines is given a prompt, which reminds him/her what to say; a prompt brings forth an action.
3. A motive is something that moves someone to act in a certain way.

Words in Context
1. incentive
2. catalyst
3. stimulus
4. motive

Page 26
Sentences may vary. Accept reasonable responses.
1. B
2. B
3. B
4. A
5. B

Page 27
Answers will vary based on students' personal experiences.

Page 29
Context Clues
1. loneliness
2. goal
3. endure
4. determination
5. opponents
6. hardy
7. weariness
8. rugged
9. victory
10. overcome

Challenge Yourself
Answers will vary. Suggested responses are provided.
1. to make a good grade in math, to join choir
2. soccer games, TV game shows

Page 30
Synonyms
1. smooth
2. weak
3. end
4. fail
5. start
6. failure
7. teammates
8. strength

Dictionary Skills
1. determination: great willpower in doing something
2. goal: something wished for; aim
3. hardy: tough; able to put up with hard conditions
4. loneliness: being alone and wanting to be with others
5. opponents: people you are competing against in a contest
6. overcome: to get the better of; to win over
7. victory: a win; success
8. weariness: tiredness; worn-out feeling

Page 31
Analogies
1. victory
2. opponents
3. determination
4. weariness
5. loneliness

Writing Sentences
Sentences will vary.

Page 32
Across
2. overcome
5. rugged
8. determination
10. opponents

Down
1. loneliness
3. weariness
4. hardy
6. endure
7. victory
9. goal

Page 33
1. B
2. C
3. D
4. C
5. D
6. A
7. B
8. C
9. A
10. A

Page 34
Answers will vary. Accept reasonable responses.

Page 35
1. I ran a little farther each day to build up my stamina before the marathon.
2. Everyone wants to be around Sally because she is full of vim.
3. Drowsiness is not uncommon after long trips.
4. Energetic people typically lead active lifestyles.
5. Sturdiness is an important physical characteristic of most football players.
6. After my friends spent the night, my room was completely discombobulated.

Page 36
1. stamina
2. judo
3. ballot
4. Fahrenheit
5. planet
6. chandelier
7. Patriotism
8. pilgrim
9. ranch
10. umbrella

Page 37
Answers will vary based on students' personal experiences.

Page 40
Context Clues
1. mortals
2. reel
3. captive
4. overtook
5. draft
6. vaguely
7. uplifted
8. veered
9. imprisoned
10. sustained

Challenge Yourself
Answers will vary. Sample answers are provided.
1. people, animals
2. jail, castle

Page 41
Synonyms
1. held
2. supported
3. drink
4. whirl

5. shift
6. raised

Antonyms
1. vaguely
2. overtook
3. veered
4. imprisoned
5. mortals
6. reel

Page 42
1. out by the other
2. Icarus paid no attention to his father's warnings.
3. snowflakes
4. He fell like a leaf tossed down by the wind. Icarus felt himself sustained, like a halcyon bird in the hollow of a wave, like a child uplifted by his mother.
5. Metaphors will vary but should compare Icarus or Daedalus to something else without using the words *like* or *as*.

Page 43
1. D
2. A
3. B
4. D
5. A
6. C
7. C
8. D
9. B
10. A

Page 44
1. After a few minutes, the courageous man left the scene.
   The lionhearted man soon departed.
2. The one thing that Sir Sneed was very good at was being brave and noble.
   Sir Sneed had a talent for being gallant.
3. There is no doubt that he is fearless.
   It's doubtless that he's dauntless.
4. Marcus was brave and bold. He would swim across the river. He was glad the water was lukewarm.
   Marcus was intrepid, and the water was tepid.
5. The large, gray mammal bravely defended her calf from the hungry lions.
   She was a valiant elephant.

Page 45
1. chivalrous
2. indomitable
3. mettlesome
4. dauntless, lionhearted, valiant, gallant, intrepid

Sample answers are provided below, but items may have more than one correct response.

5. chivalrous
6. lionhearted
7. mettlesome
8. intrepid
9. dauntless
10. valiant
11. indomitable
12. gallant

Page 46
1. meddlesome
2. mettlesome
3. indomitable
4. abominable
5. gallant
6. gallon
7. valance
8. valiant
9. chivalry
10. shivery

Page 47
Answers will vary based on students' personal experiences.

Page 49
Context Clues
1. dedicated
2. instructed
3. assignment; capsule
4. liftoff
5. commander

6. gravitational
7. sensation
8. cockpit
9. aerial

Challenge Yourself
Answers will vary. Sample answers are provided.
1. oceans, continents
2. stock shelves, deliver a package

Page 50
Word Sense
New phrases will vary. Accept reasonable responses.
1. no
2. yes
3. yes
4. no
5. no
6. yes
7. no
8. yes
9. no
10. no

Synonyms
1. devoted
2. feeling
3. chief
4. taught
5. job

Page 51
Across
4. gravitational
7. dedicated
8. commander
9. capsule
10. cockpit

Down
1. liftoff
2. instructed
3. sensation
5. assignment
6. aerial

Page 52
Related Words
1. command; commander
2. assign; assignment
3. gravity; gravitational
4. instructions; instructed
5. dedication; dedicated
6. sense; sensation

Writing Sentences
Sentences will vary.

Page 53
1. C
2. A
3. A
4. C
5. B
6. B
7. D
8. B
9. C

Page 54
Greek Roots
1. E
2. C
3. A
4. B
5. D

Answers will vary for items 6 and 7. Sample responses are provided.
6. relating to the air
7. spectacular flying stunts

Compare and Contrast
1. Acrobatics is like gymnastics except that acrobatics often involve being high up.
2. Calisthenics is like ballet because both involve graceful movements.
3. Asteroids are like meteoroids except that asteroids are larger.

Page 55
Answers will vary. Accept reasonable responses.
1. types of physical exercise; aerobics
2. root *aero*; aerial
3. root *naut*; nautilus
4. words with *space*; spacecraft
5. base word *gym*; gymnast
6. vital organs; liver, kidneys
7. physical activity; rowing, hiking
8. weather conditions; sunny
9. games played on a court; tennis
10. wheeled objects; bicycle

Page 56
1. NASA
2. NATO
3. UNICEF
4. PBS
5. OPEC
6. SCUBA
7. POW
8. SOS
9. WHO
10. AWOL
11. ASAP
12. ROM
13. ZIP
14. RAM
15. HQ

Page 57
Answers will vary based on students' personal experiences.

Page 59
1. influence
2. barrier
3. equality
4. courageous
5. superb
6. fielder
7. popularity
8. athletic
9. recognition
10. prejudice

Page 60
Related Words
1. athlete; athletic
2. recognize; recognition
3. popular; popularity
4. courage; courageous
5. equal; equality
6. superbly; superb

Writing Sentences
Sentences will vary.

Page 61
1. athletic
2. fielder
3. popularity
4. barrier
5. equality
6. courageous
7. influence
8. superb
9. prejudice
10. recognition

Page 62
Word Sense
New phrases will vary. Accept reasonable responses.
1. yes
2. no
3. yes
4. no
5. yes
6. no
7. yes
8. no
9. no
10. no

Word Pairs
Sentences will vary. Accept reasonable responses.

Page 63
1. A
2. B
3. D
4. D
5. C
6. A
7. D
8. B
9. B
10. A

Page 64
1. viewpoint, outlook
2. ideas, beliefs
3. unbiased, fair
4. likeness, image
5. opinion, point of view
6. imperfect, blemished
7. blanket, coverlet
8. factual
9. serious
10. unfinished, incomplete
11. impartial
12. bland, tasteless
13. fact
14. professional
15. build, establish

Page 65
Sentences will vary. Accept reasonable

responses.
1. B
2. A
3. A
4. B
5. B

Page 66
Accept reasonable responses.

Page 67
Answers will vary based on students' personal experiences.

Page 69
1. organization
2. adulthood
3. bustle
4. teeming
5. tireless
6. cooperate
7. existence
8. authority
9. threat
10. defend

Page 70
Writing Sentences
Sentences will vary.

Cloze Paragraphs
1. defend
2. threat
3. cooperate
4. teeming
5. bustle
6. authority

Page 71
Answers will vary. Accept reasonable responses.
1. Jobs of Worker Ants: defend
2. Ways Ants Act: cooperate, bustle, tireless
3. About the Ant Colony Queen: organization, authority

Page 72
Word Sense
New phrases will vary. Accept reasonable responses.
1. no
2. yes
3. no
4. yes
5. no
6. no
7. no
8. yes

Challenge Yourself
Answers will vary. Suggested responses are provided.
1. Girl/Boy scouts, 4-H Club
2. teacher, police officer
3. take turns, share

Page 73
1. C
2. B
3. B
4. D
5. A
6. C
7. C
8. A
9. B
10. D

Page 74
1. fascinating
2. patronizing
3. continuing
4. restraining
5. dazzling
6. inspiring
7. astonishing
8. attracting
9. overwhelming
10. accelerating
11. compelling
12. recuperating
13. nauseating
14. beguiling
15. captivating
16. charming

Answers may vary slightly. Accept reasonable responses.
17. accelerating
18. nauseating
19. dazzling
20. inspiring or astonishing
21. compelling
22. fascinating
23. recuperating

24. continuing
25. attracting

Page 75
Answers may vary. Accept reasonable responses.
1. full or crowded
2. pleasing or delightful
3. extremely interesting
4. amazing or surprising
5. filled with thought or feeling
6. charming or pleasing
7. fascinating or charming
8. demanding of attention
9. shining
10. amazing

Page 76
1. fascinating, ordinary
2. recall, forget
3. attracting, repelling
4. brief, lengthy
5. sturdy, fragile
6. astonishing, expected
7. decline, accept
8. frisky, lazy
9. local, distant
10. amateur, professional
11. problem, solution
12. compelling, boring
13. shaky, firm
14. captivating, dull
15. anxiety, confidence

Page 77
Answers will vary based on students' personal experiences.

Page 79
1. behavior
2. specialize
3. victims
4. devour
5. conceal
6. attract
7. poisonous
8. digest
9. paralyzed
10. attentive

Page 80
Word Groups
1. poisonous
2. devour
3. conceal
4. behavior
5. attentive
6. paralyzed
7. attract
8. specialize

Challenge Yourself
Answers will vary. Suggested responses are provided.
1. snakes, mushrooms
2. peanut butter, popcorn
3. closet, under the bed

Page 81
Word Sense
New phrases will vary. Accept reasonable responses.
1. no
2. no
3. yes
4. yes
5. no
6. no
7. yes
8. no
9. yes
10. no

Word Pairs
Sentences will vary. Accept reasonable responses.

Page 82
1. **artist/dip**
   attentive
   attract
   behavior
   conceal
   devour
   digest
2. **pal/queen**
   paralyzed
   poisonous
3. **rabbit/when**
   specialize
   victims

Sentences for 4. to 6. will vary.

Page 83
1. D
2. B
3. C
4. A
5. A
6. D
7. B
8. C
9. B
10. D

Page 84
Answers may vary. Possible responses are given.
2. base word *herb*, add herbalist
3. prefix *omni-*, add omnivorous
4. root *vor*, add omnivore
5. root *rave*, add ravening
6. root *aqua*, add aquamarine
7. prefix *astro-*, add astronaut
8. prefix *bio-*, add biodome
9. prefix *trans-*, add transportation
10. suffix *-able*, add laughable

Page 85
Answers may vary slightly.
1. plants
2. drink
3. humans
4. insects
5. contrast
6. spectators
7. bones
8. lava
9. lungs
10. final
11. tired
12. desert
13. writer
14. time
15. take

Page 86
2. gently
3. homeward
4. carnivorous
5. herbivorous
6. omnivorous
7. childhood
8. teacher
9. quietly
10. golden

Page 87
Answers will vary based on students' personal experiences.

Page 89
Context Clues
1. horizontal
2. encircle
3. cobwebs
4. fragile
5. diameter
6. suspends
7. vertical
8. circular
9. rectangles
10. flexible

Challenge Yourself
Answers will vary. Suggested responses are provided.
1. glass, baby
2. balloon, light fixture

Page 90
1. fragile
2. cobwebs
3. rectangles
4. flexible
5. circular
6. suspends

Writing Sentences
Sentences will vary.

Page 91
1. encircle
2. vertical
3. flexible
4. rectangles
5. cobwebs
6. horizontal
7. suspends
8. fragile

Answer: Because they're good at catching flies!

Page 92
Sentences will vary.
1. no
2. no
3. yes
4. yes
5. no
6. no
7. no
8. yes
9. no

Page 93
1. B
2. A
3. C
4. D
5. B
6. A
7. B
8. A
9. D
10. C

Page 94
1. facade
2. foundation
3. gargoyle
4. cornerstone
5. edifice
6. architect
7. Gothic
8. architecture

Answers may vary slightly.
9. houses, museums, skyscrapers, office buildings, courthouses
10. The foundation is the most important part of the building because it supports the building.

Page 95
Answers may vary slightly.
1. parts of a building
2. tall buildings
3. professions
4. kinds of handicrafts
5. kinds of building materials
6. styles of architecture

Additional words may vary.
7. cross out texture; add architecture
8. cross out dessert; add designing
9. cross out bulletin; add building
10. cross out conifer; add constructing
11. cross out tandem; add transportation
12. cross out credit; add creating

Page 96
Answers may vary.
1. both involve designing and creating
2. both are very tall buildings
3. architecture is the design of buildings and construction is the building of them
4. gargoyles also contain a channel for draining water
5. both are styles of architecture
6. both are types of supports
7. both provide information about how to do something
8. both cover the front of something
9. both are passageways used to bypass bodies of water or other obstacles
10. both can be used to help you find your way

Page 97
Answers will vary based on students' personal experiences.

Page 99
Context Clues
1. viewers
2. version
3. dependable
4. clashed
5. alien
6. fascination
7. villains
8. ambitious
9. elaborate
10. galaxies

Challenge Yourself
Answers will vary. Suggested responses are provided.
1. at a movie, at a baseball game
2. Dracula, Catwoman

Page 100
Antonyms
1. elaborate
2. fascination
3. dependable
4. ambitious
5. alien

Rewriting Sentences
1. I have always wanted to visit other galaxies.
2. I would take along my dependable robot.
3. We would fight and conquer many villains.
4. I could write a book and then make the movie version.

Page 101
Related Words
1. fascinated; fascination
2. view; viewers
3. elaborately; elaborate
4. depends; dependable

5. ambition; ambitious

Word Sense
New phrases will vary.
1. yes
2. no
3. no
4. yes

Page 102
Across
4. elaborate
6. alien
7. version
8. clashed
9. ambitious

Down
1. galaxies
2. dependable
3. villains
5. fascination
7. viewers

Page 103
1. B
2. D
3. B
4. A
5. C
6. D
7. A
8. D
9. C
10. B

Page 104
Answers will vary. Accept reasonable responses.
1. both involve creating things
2. manufactured involves producing materials with machines
3. artistry suggests creativity
4. both involve physical ability or grace
5. expertise suggests more in-depth knowledge
6. both involve using the hands
7. both mean "skill or aptitude"

Answers to the questions will vary.

Page 105
Additional words may vary. Accept reasonable responses.

1. D; skill
2. A; handwriting
3. B; manicure
4. B; artistic
5. D; touch
6. C; inventive
7. B; create
8. D; sewing
9. C; coordination
10. B; experienced

Page 106
Additional words may vary. Accept reasonable responses.

1. Examples of Handicrafts: pottery; woodworking; needlepoint
2. Things That Are Manufactured: plastic containers; automobiles; machinery
3. Sports That Require Dexterity: tennis; basketball; golf
4. Activities That Require Artistry: drawing; sculpting; painting
5. Sample answer: Artistic activities require dexterity. Artists need skilled hands to paint, draw, or sculpt.

Page 107
Answers will vary based on students' personal experiences.

CPSIA information can be obtained
at www.ICGtesting.com
Printed in the USA
BVHW020150280623
666457BV00009B/47